terminals	operator/ownership	modalsplit passengers % 1999

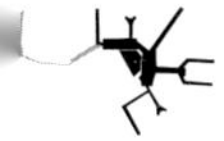

Schiphol Group
75.8% state-owned
21.8% City of Amsterdam
2.4% City of Rotterdam

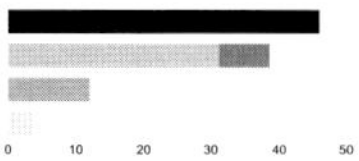
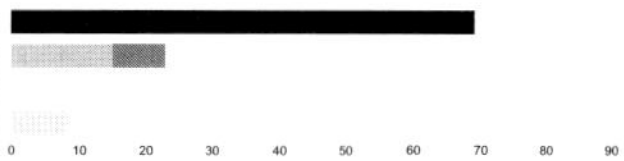

car	46	68.6
train/bus	31 / 7	14.8 / 7.9
taxi	12	0
other	4	8.7

AMS

SCAA
100% state-owned

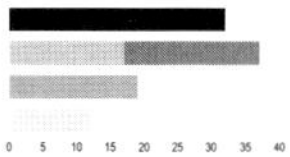
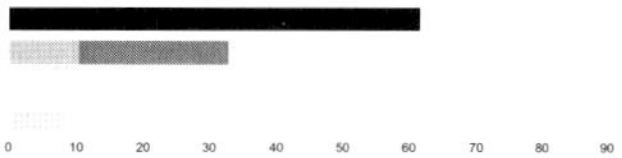

car	32	60
train/bus	17 / 20	10 / 22
taxi	19	0
other	12	8

ARN

AENA
100% state-owned

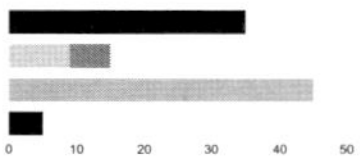
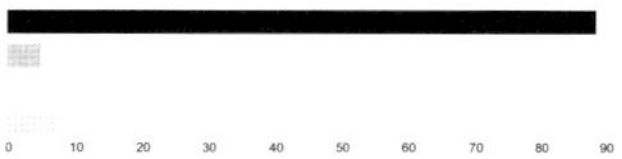

car	45	88
train/bus	9 / 6	5 / 0
taxi	35	0
other	5	7

BCN

AdP (Aéroports de Paris)
100% state-owned

not covered

not covered

CDG

FRAPORT (Frankfurt Airport)
45.2% Land Hessen
28.9% City of Frankfurt
25.9% Germany

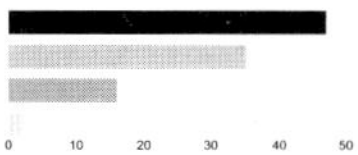
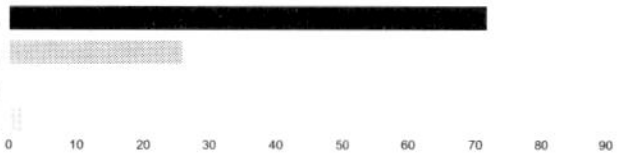

car	47	72
train/bus	35	26
taxi	16	0
other	2	2

FRA

Editorial Gustavo Gili, SA
08029 Barcelona Rosselló, 87-89. Tel. 93 322 81 61

from airport to airport city

Güller Güller

GG

This book is in part based on research carried out in 2000 by the authors for the European Airport Regions Conference ARC.

Graphic design: Jordi Lascorz
Text revision: Paul Hammond

Printed in Spain
ISBN: 84-252-1905-1
Printing: EGEDSA, Sabadell (Barcelona)

Contents

Foreword

Jordi Julià Sort

Barcelona Regional, Metropolitan Agency
for Urbanism and Infrastructures
Chairman of the Airport Regions
Conference's Transport Working Group

Bob Verburg

Province of Noord-Holland
President of the ARC

Airports have become key facilities for the competitiveness of any territory. A good airport is a precondition for a region to play a major role in the current global economy. Airports are huge generators of economic activity, but also important sources of environmental problems. The Airports Regions Conference (ARC), founded in 1994, is a forum where more than twenty European local and regional authorities share their experiences in these areas, by organising debates, conferences and working group meetings. Mathis and Michael Güller have undertaken an investigation for the ARC on the relationship between land use and transport at and around airports. This research has shed light on, and outlined in detail, two of the main territorial consequences of the spectacular growth of airports: the trend of airports to develop "airport cities" around themselves, and their configuration as "intermodal transport nodes" at the metropolitan or regional level. These functions go beyond what airports were traditionally meant to be: highly specialised "air transport factories", often ruled by "civil" administrations of military origin. Nowadays, airport operators, more often than not private companies, are exploiting their location's potential through real estate developments and the management of commercial centres. But at the same time airport operators act as authorities in the field of transport, with enormous influence in the region's air connections, and by creating road networks and AiRail terminals. There is an overlap of functions between airports and other institutions, and often —even in those cases where these institutions participate in the ownership of the airport— conflicts of interest arise. An understanding of this complex process is the first step to solving such conflicts. Regional and local authorities, with their expertise and responsibilities in the fields of city and transport planning, have to play a crucial role in this process. The work of Güller Güller is a major contribution to preparing the ground for the active involvement of local and regional institutions. We are sure this knowledge will be of use to many of the other agencies involved, and therefore welcome the publication of this book.

Introduction

Jack Short

Secretary General
European Conference of Ministers of Transport

Aviation is Europe's fastest growing transport mode, with long-run average annual traffic increases of over 6%. Following the horrific events of 11 September 2001, traffic went down for the first time in a decade. Despite this, the underlying trends are reasserting themselves, boosted by factors like the emergence and rapid growth of low-cost airlines. Indeed, the forecast that air traffic in Europe will double by 2015 remains a reasonable basis for policy formulation.

Providing adequate airport capacity to deal with this traffic is a serious challenge. Capacity has been increasing, though at a slower rate than demand. This is not surprising, as airports bring dramatic changes to land use and have major adverse environmental effects. The assessment, planning and construction of new facilities is a controversial and increasingly lengthy process.

Airports are no longer just airports, as the book strikingly observes. But what are they? Nodes of a new intermodal transport system for both people and goods? New cities, with shopping, hotels, conferences and a host of ancillary activities more or less loosely linked to aviation? New sprawling developments gobbling up precious land? Unlived-in new cities with serious congestion, access, noise and pollution problems? Dynamic centres of economic activity and growth at the heart of a network of high-speed links to other centres? To varying degrees airports are all of these things. Originally conceived and built as stand-alone facilities outside towns, they have changed and are changing beyond recognition. Now, in many airports most of the people are not taking a plane at all. Airports have become major centres of employment and sites for business contacts, as well as vital logistic and distribution centres. Much of this just happened without a clear planning framework, and these multifunctional airports have often been poorly integrated into regional and local transport plans, resulting in ongoing disputes with local authorities and residents and increasingly difficult access problems. As it is, the trip to the airport often lasts longer than the flight one will eventually take. Moving about within these vast complexes is frequently difficult and slow. An emerging issue concerns secondary airports, which are also growing fast, partly to cater for low-cost airlines, but posing their own problems of access and costs.

In summary, there is a wide variety of policy challenges involving airports. These include strategic and development planning issues, providing adequate access, especially for public transport, serious problems of pricing and charging for the use of facilities and numerous local and wider environmental problems, all of which are of a particularly real and urgent kind. Indeed, airports pose some of the clearest practical challenges to achieving the right balance between the economic, social and environmental aims that sustainability demands. The specific challenge for airports to harness the positive developmental features and minimise the harmful and wasteful ones is at the heart of the broad debate on transport and its sustainability.

This book shows concretely that there are new ideas on many of these subjects, and that different governments and regional and local authorities are grappling with the complex array of interacting issues. There is no one model for how airports can best be integrated into a coherent spatial planning framework, nor for how access to them and within them can best be provided. This book shows how some embrace the airport city concept warmly, while others eschew it. It shows how different planning and institutional frameworks need to be adapted to national and local circumstances. The integration of airports within a coherent framework of regional planning contains additional levels of complexity compared to traditional urban planning. This complexity arises especially in the number and variety of institutional actors involved, and bringing these together in a constructive spirit is one of the most difficult challenges.

The book demonstrates that several lessons are emerging from the reflection that is under way. Perhaps the most important is the need to have a comprehensive regional framework for land use and transport planning which fully integrates airports and their development. Another is that, while it is undisputed that airports can bring economic benefits to an urban region, more needs to be done to mitigate the great and sudden pressures they place on existing infrastructures, on local facilities and on the environment. The trend, too, for airports to increase dramatically in area shows how new concepts in airport design are needed. It has become clear that airport access that is too heavily dependent on road transport brings additional problems and is often counterproductive. Additionally, it is not just for passengers that access to and within airports needs to be planned, since goods are becoming increasingly important. Finally, there are lessons for airports in terms of the siting of different services and facilities within the airport complex. Building train connections is of little use if the stops are not near the final destinations that people want.

This stimulating book and the ideas and examples in it will contribute to a much needed reflection by national, regional and local land use and transport planners, as well as political actors and others involved in airport planning and design. Airports are vital parts of our modern fabric and their conception, planning, construction, expansion and operation need to be much better incorporated into our land use and transport policies at regional level. This book makes an important contribution to this process.

In their work and beliefs, authors Michael and Mathis Güller represent a pragmatic and adaptable form of planning that takes account of the great variety of different local circumstances and the real needs of people. They have raised an issue of great import where developing new ideas and learning from them will be essential if we are to make progress towards our sustainability goals.

NUON
Rabobank
kpn
mobile

The reality of airports is changing: adverts, real estate and green areas arise on what used to be vast car parks alone. Is that an airport city? (Schiphol Plaza in 2002).

From airport to airport city

Airports are not just airports any more. Forgoing their status as simple traffic machines in the periphery, airports have become the most decisive transport infrastructures in the transformation of the metropolitan area. Propelled by a series of strategic investments, they have assumed key positions in High Speed Train (HST), railway and light-rail networks which until recently were limited to central stations alone. Being undisputed as regional and global interfaces of the regions of Europe, airports are changing into centres of activity within them, new regional development poles or simply "airport cities".

Airport operators subscribe to new business opportunities with a stronger focus on commercial and real estate development. But the self-confidence with which many operators expand the scope of their activities is not yet reflected in airport planning. Most plans for airport cities are still designed according to the pragmatic logic of an efficient airport infrastructure.

Local and regional authorities are overwhelmed by the speed and scale of developments. They find it ever more difficult to cope with airports that now exhibit the operational and organisational needs of a city. With straightforward entrepreneurial reasoning replacing the former "public" management of airports, responsibilities between the airport operator and the surrounding authorities are anything but clear.

The present book results from a wish to collect evidence of these processes and to pinpoint and decipher two current trends within airport development: the growth of an airport city and the evolution of a landside interchange node. It does not suggest that either one or the other is inevitable, always necessary and desirable. Rather, it provides a vision of the influence of airports in rearranging landside traffic networks and in reorganising the territory of the metropolitan area. Based on insight into nine European airport regions, it develops a new framework for airport planning, one that allows for participation in the making and shaping of this most dynamic motor of urban development.

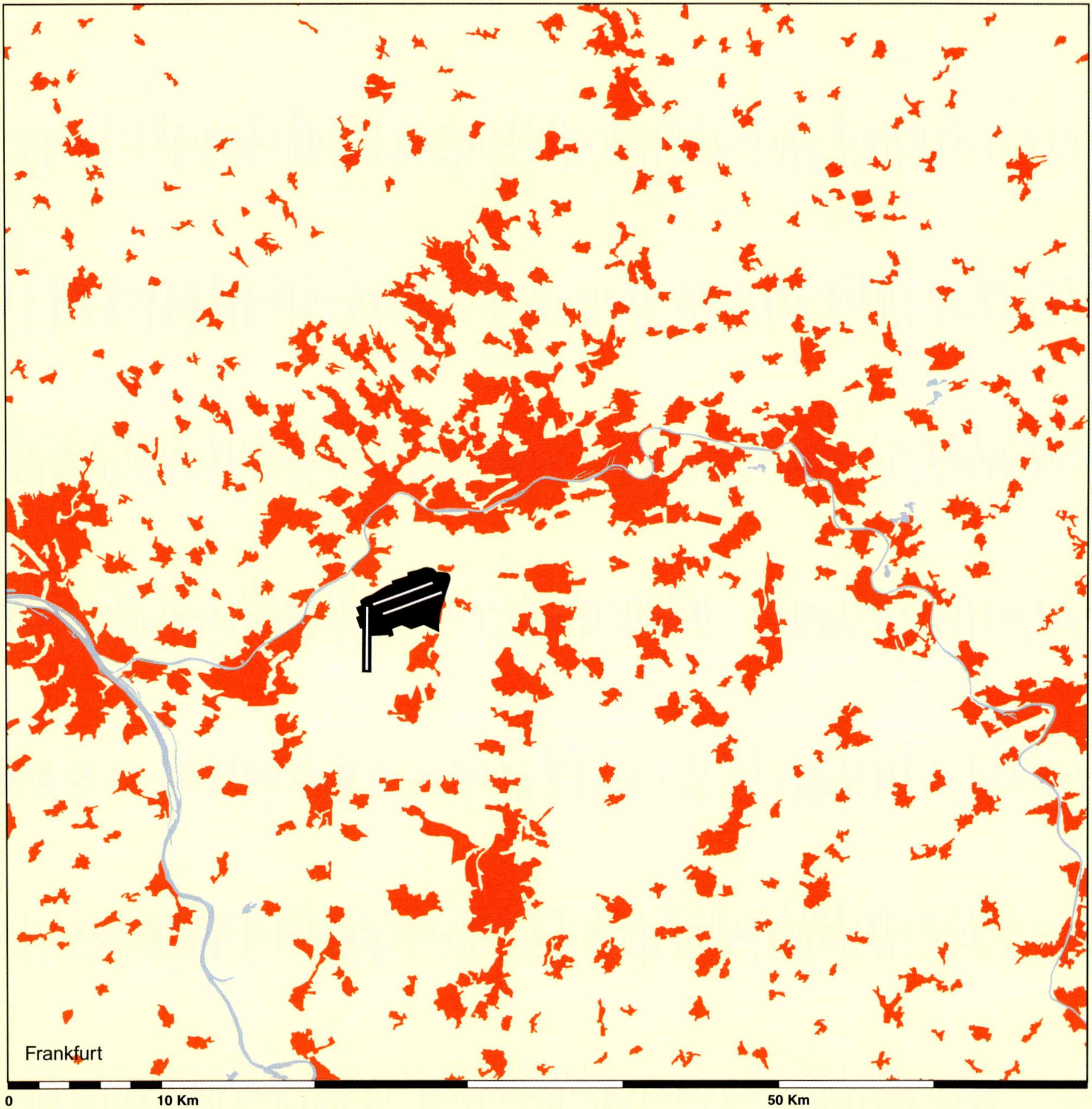

Frankfurt
0
10 Km
50 Km

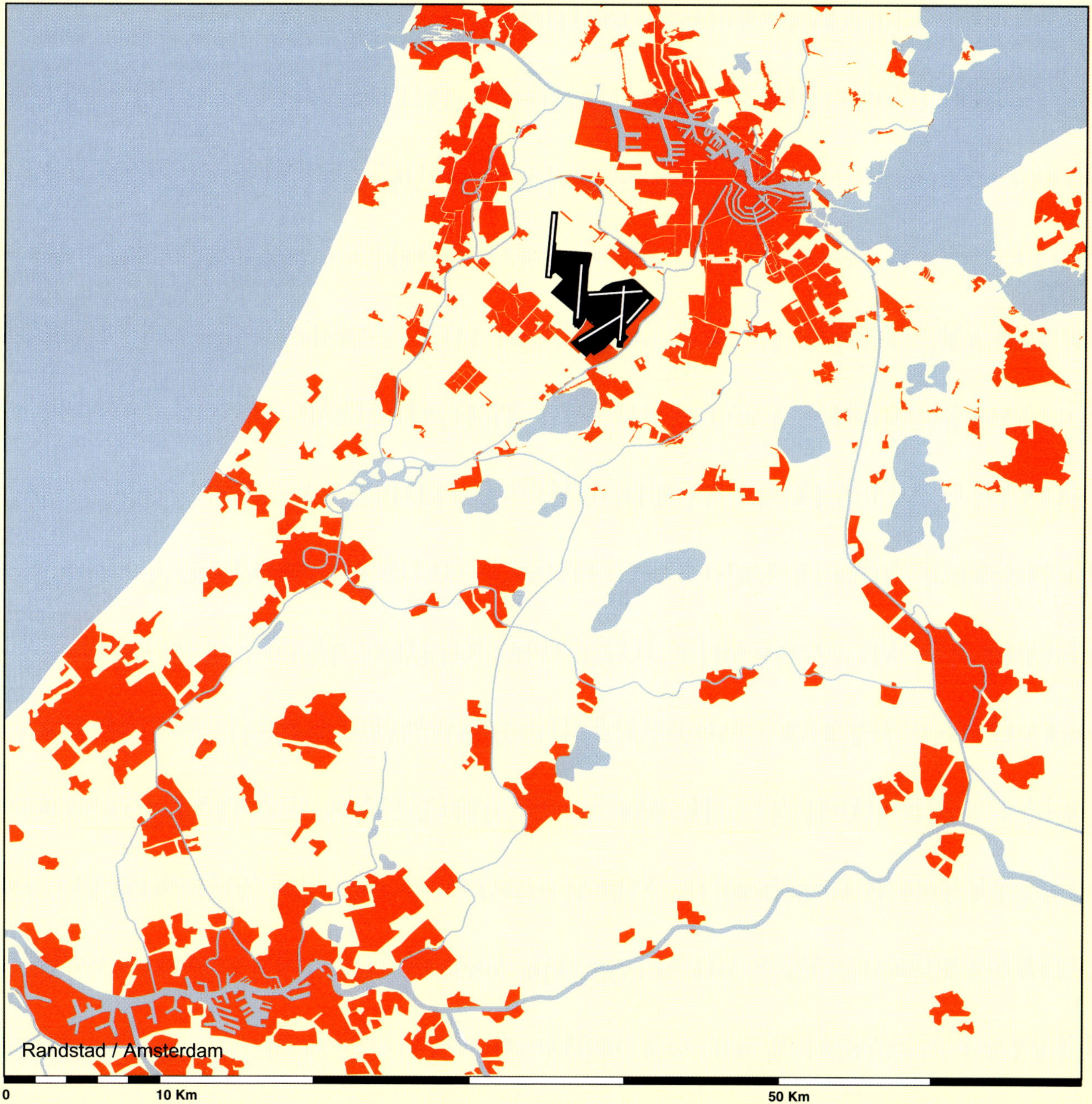
Randstad / Amsterdam
0
10 Km
50 Km

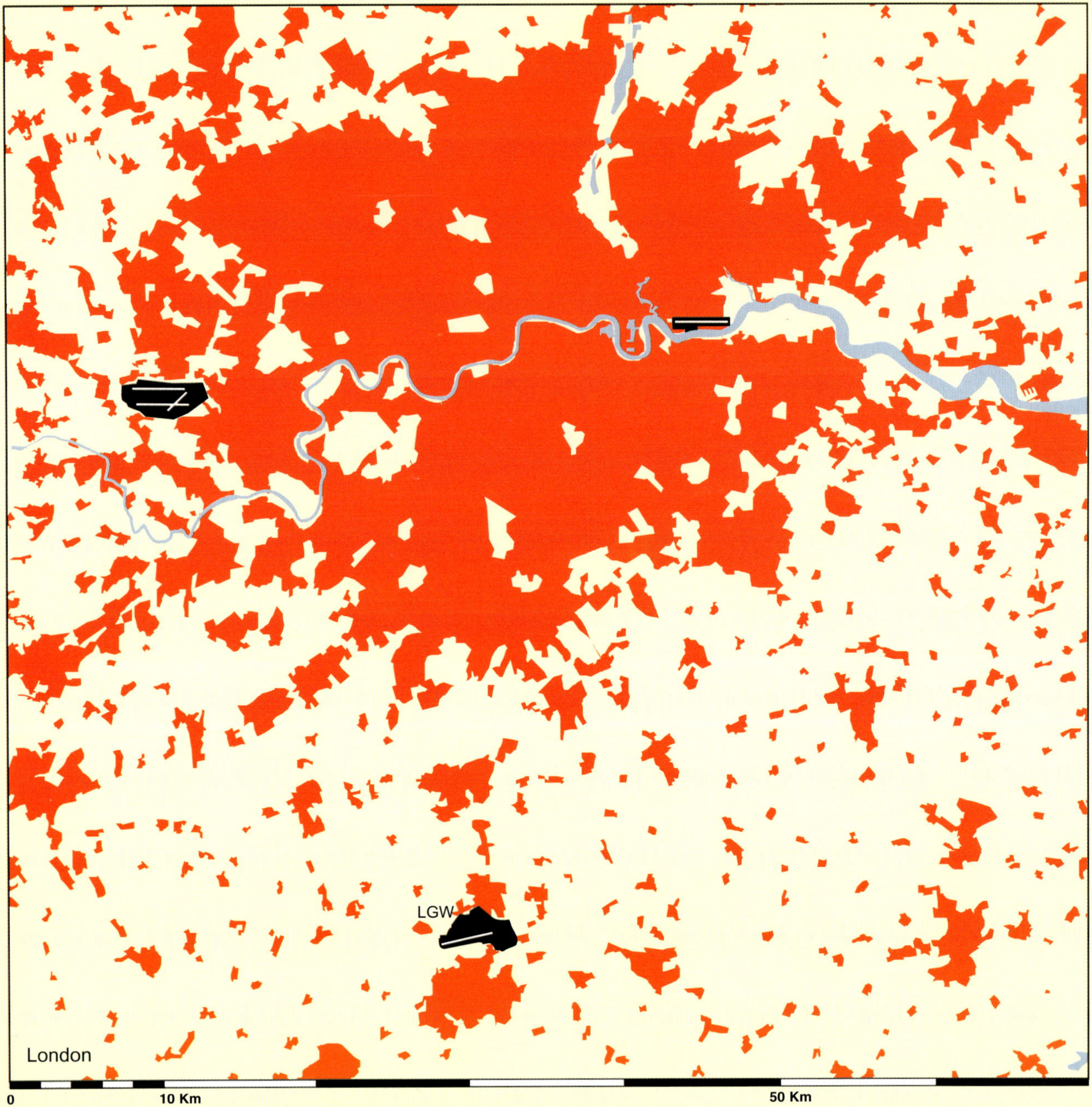
LGW
London
0
10 Km
50 Km

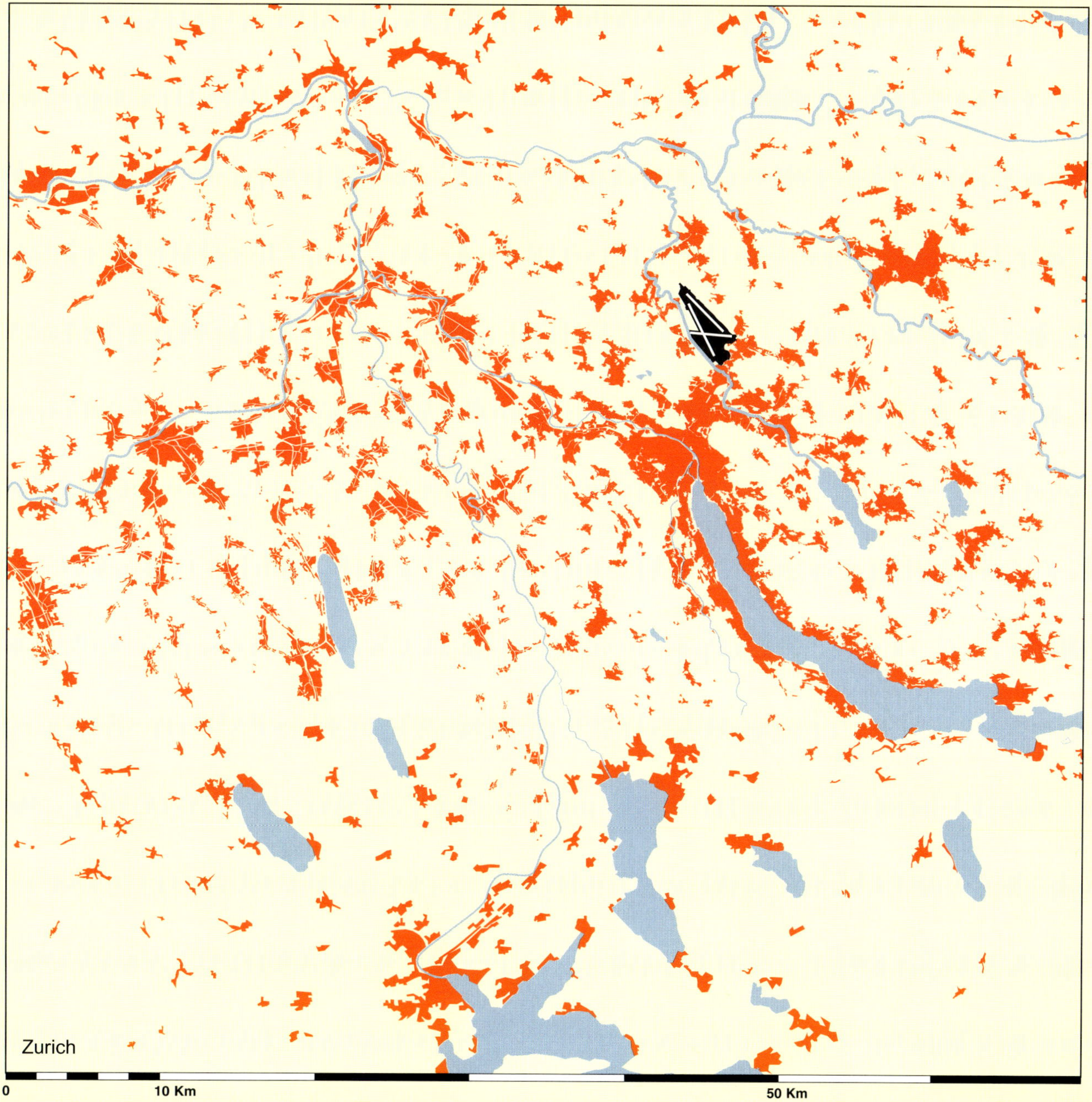
Zurich
0
10 Km
50 Km

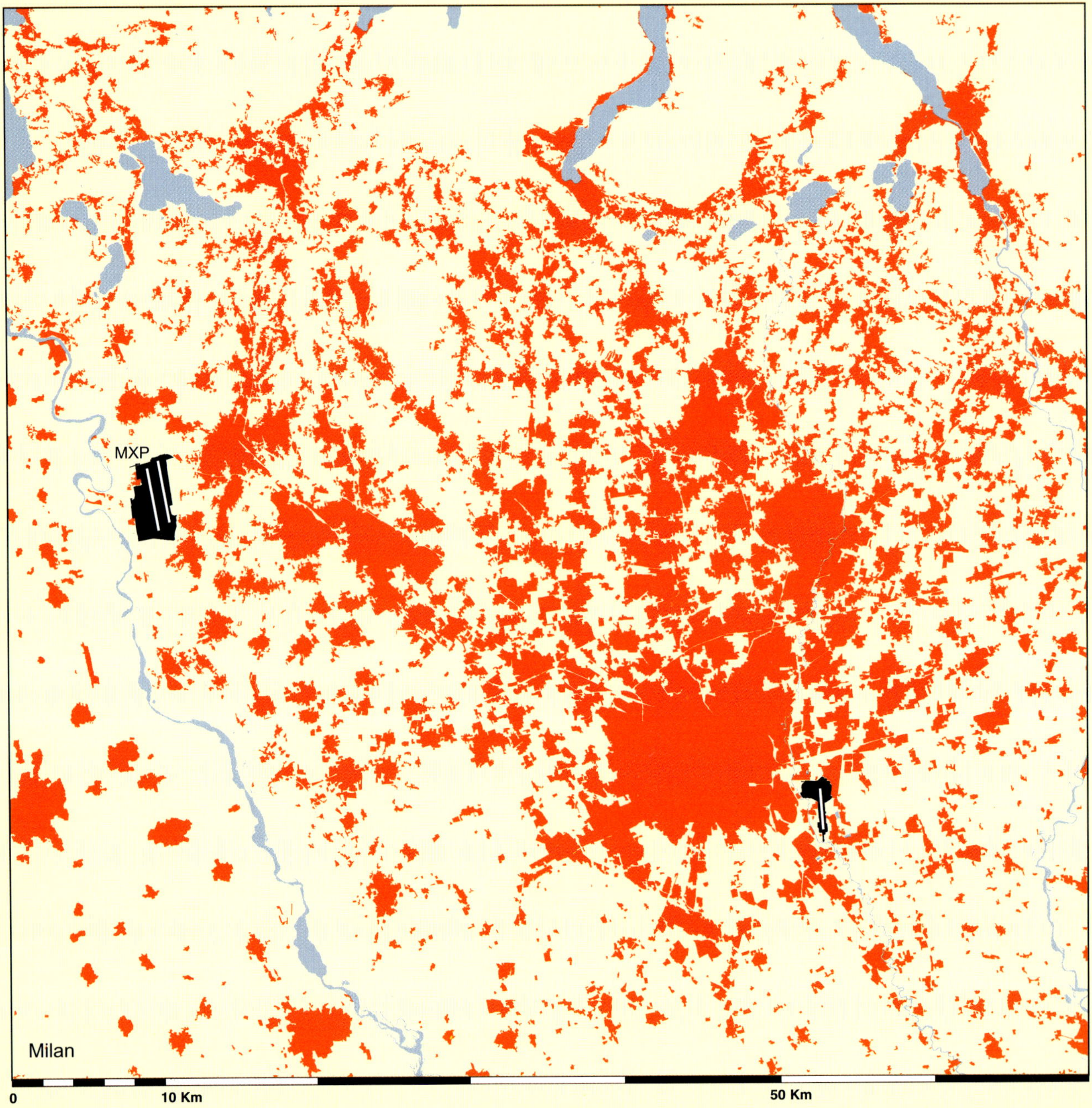
MXP
Milan
0
10 Km
50 Km

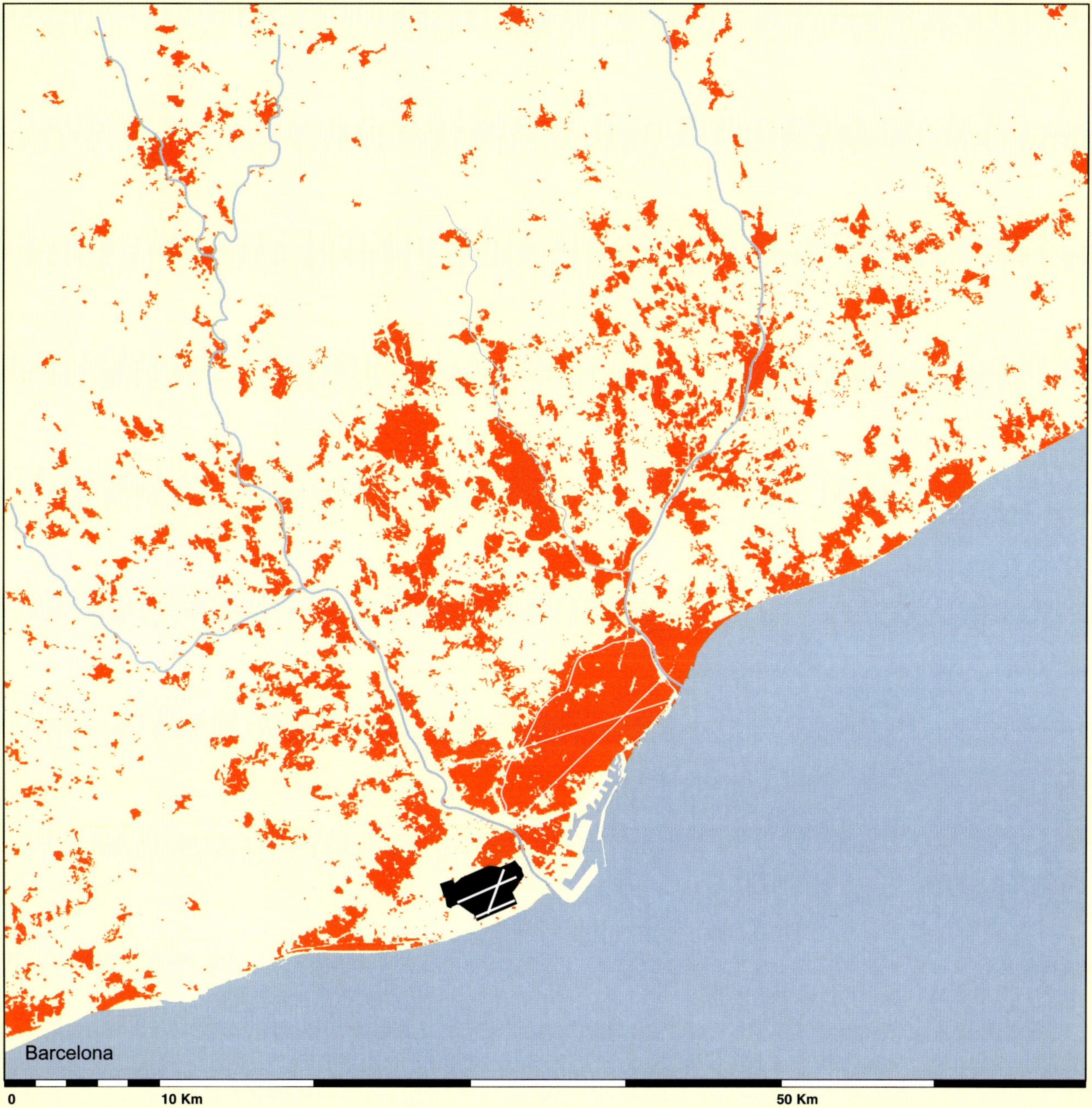
Barcelona
0
10 Km
50 Km

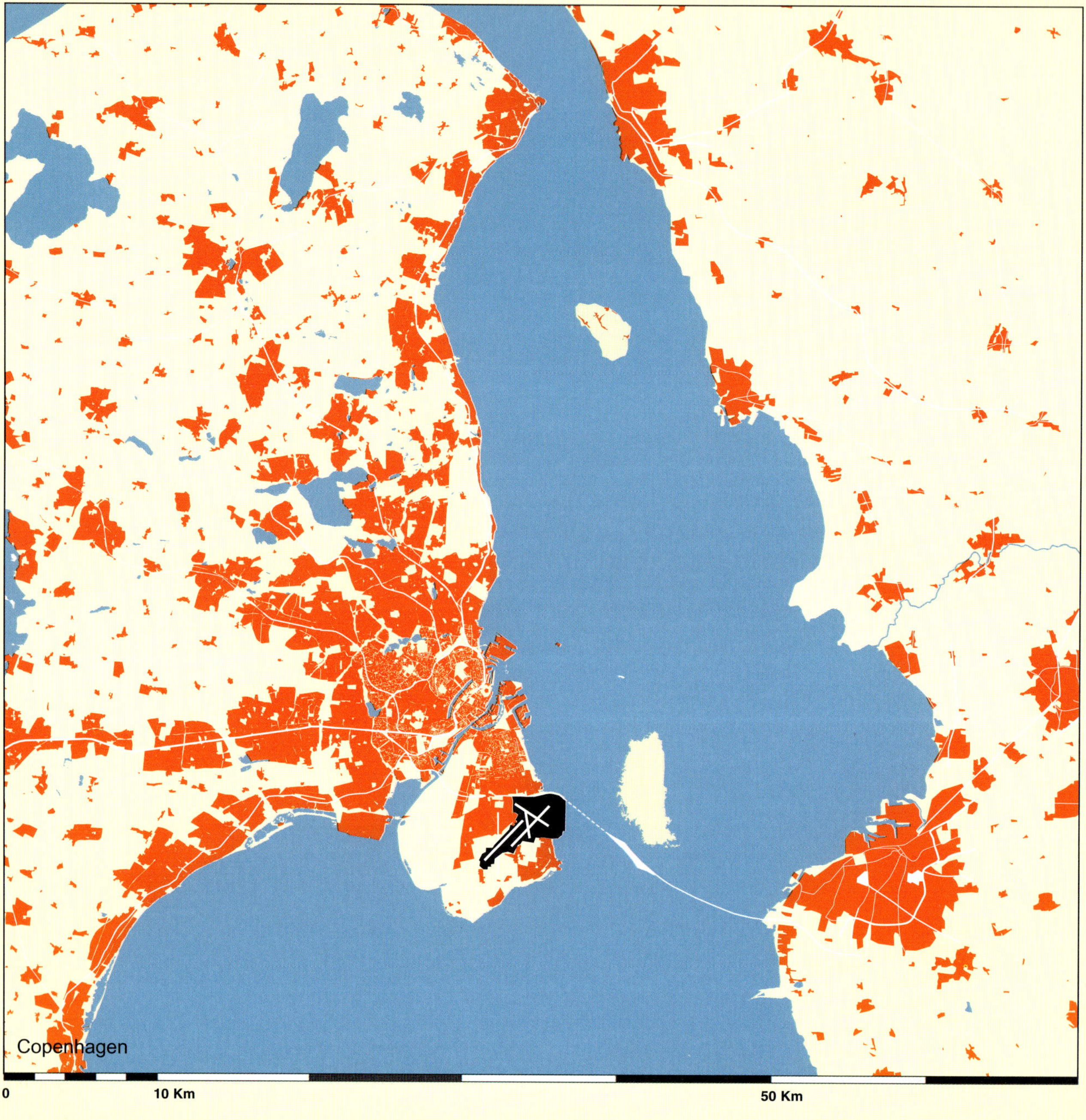
Copenhagen
0
10 Km
50 Km

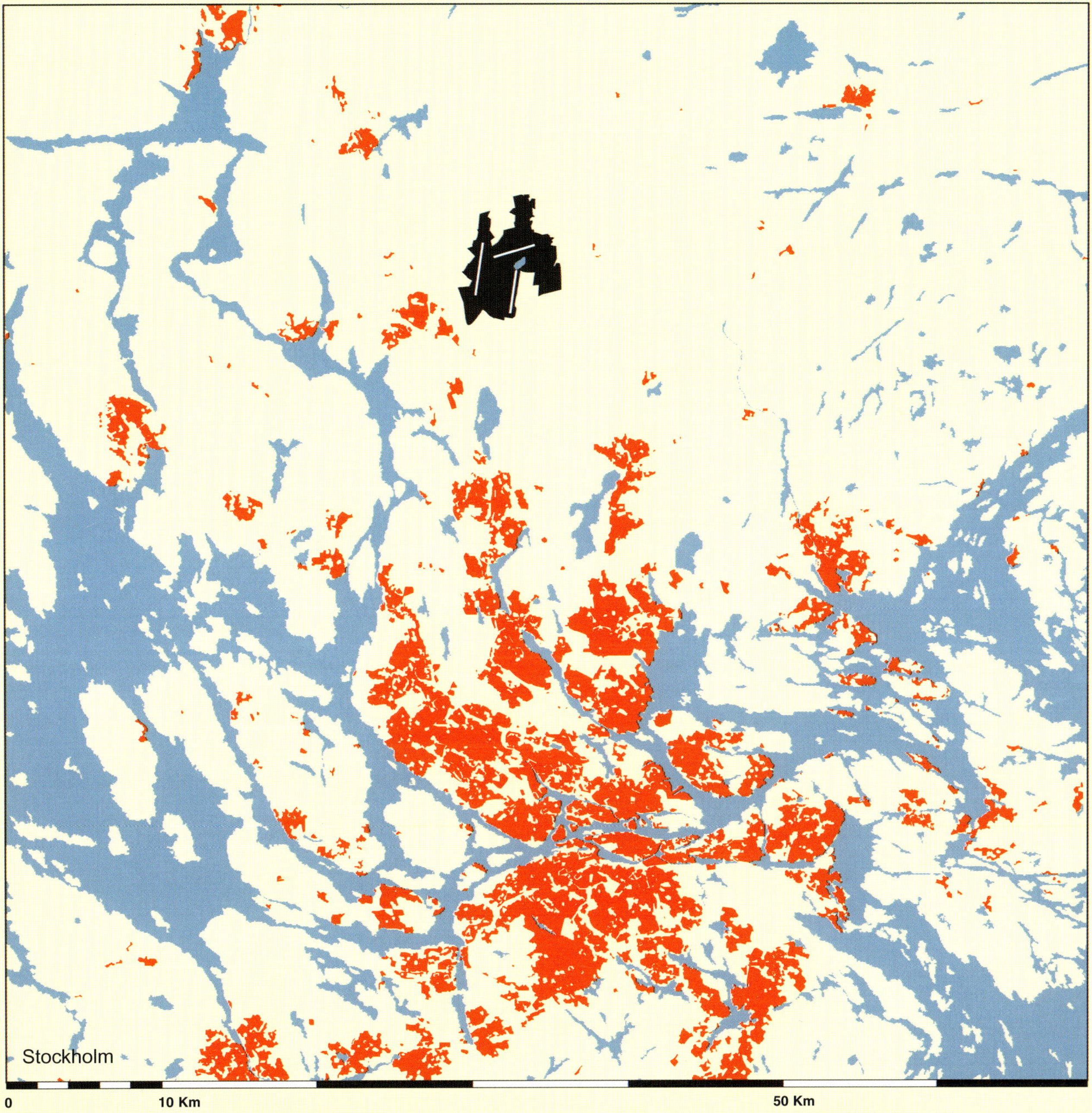
Stockholm
0
10 Km
50 Km

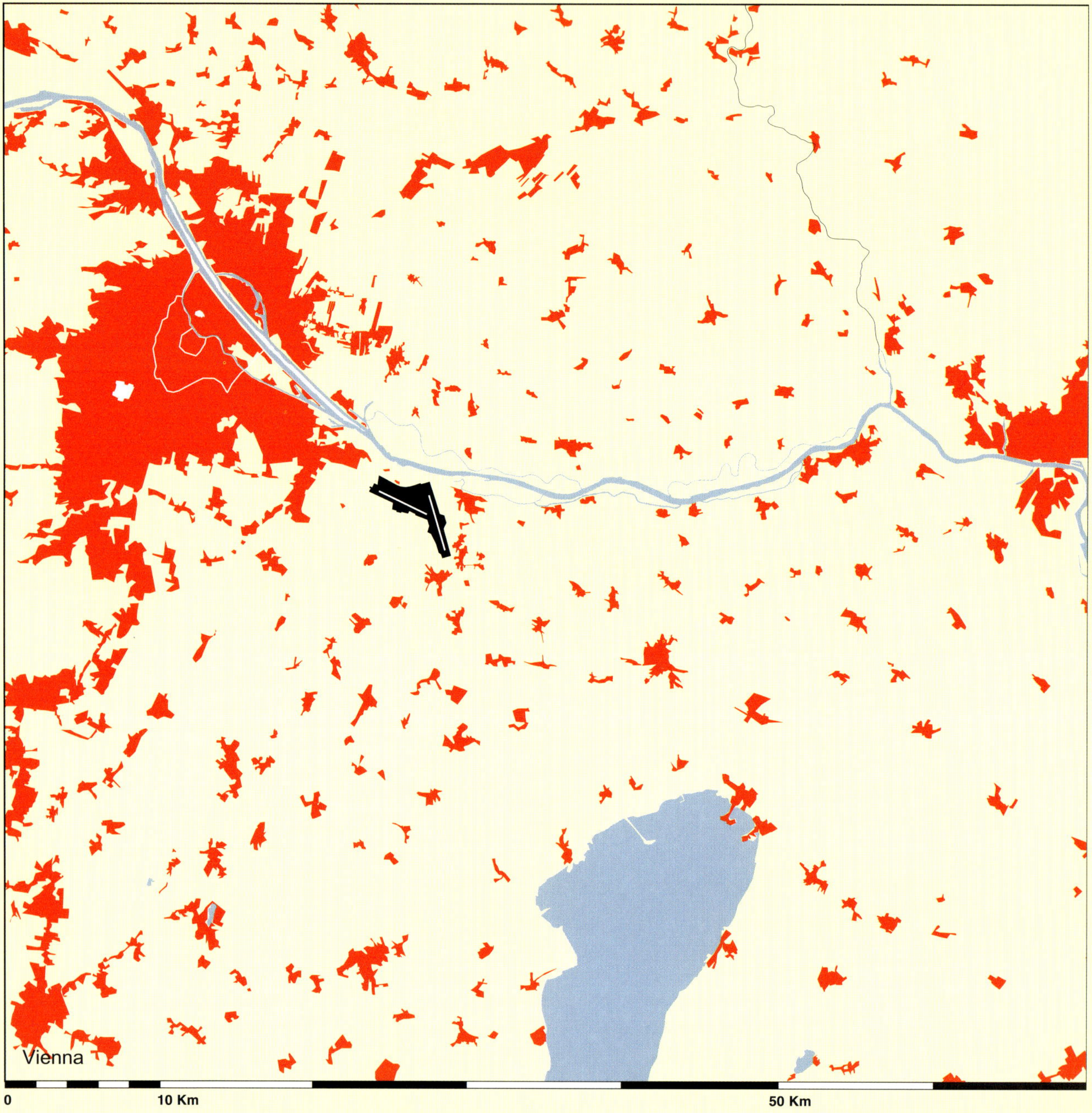
Vienna
0
10 Km
50 Km

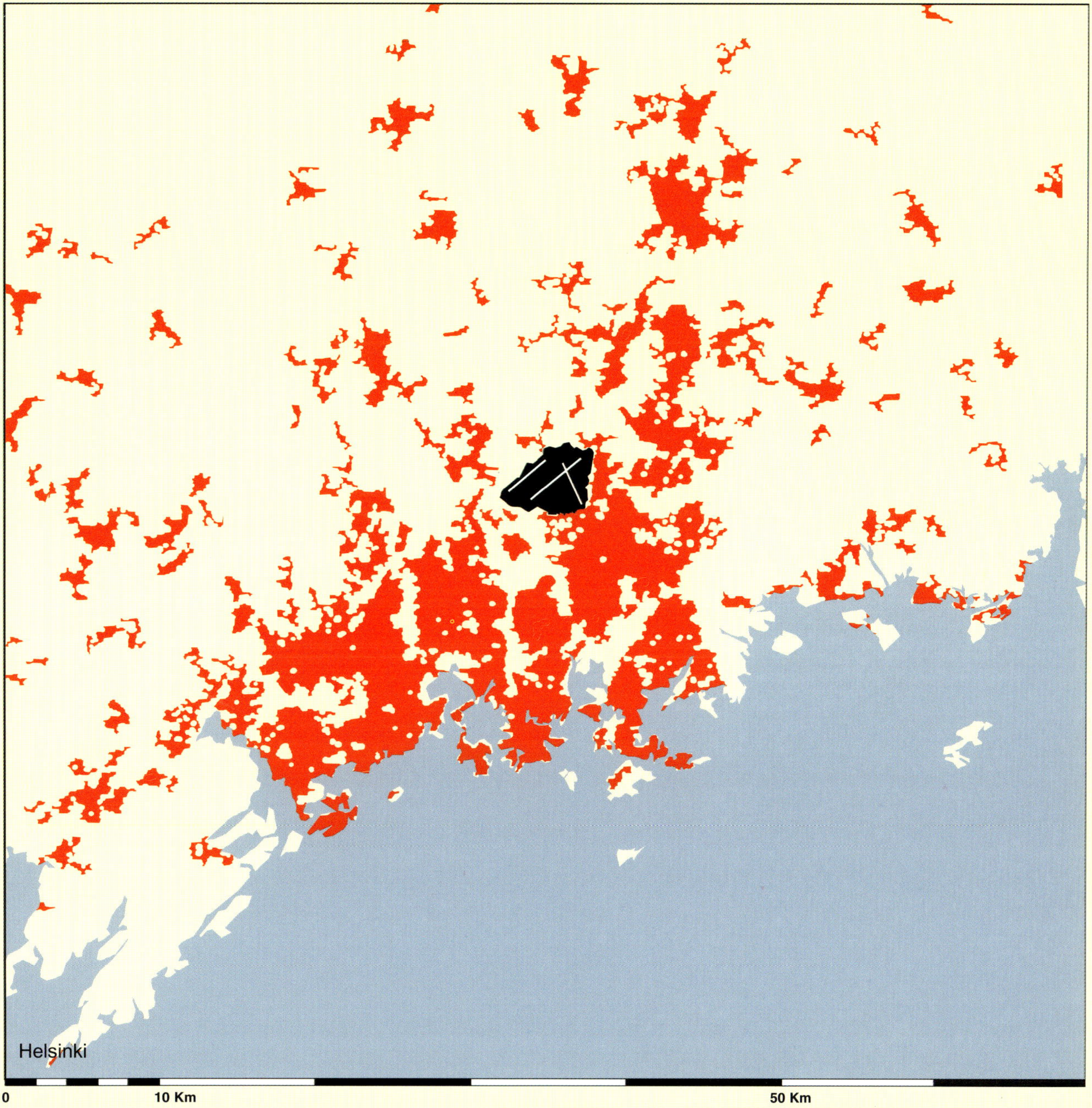
Helsinki
0
10 Km
50 Km

1. New cities at regional and global interfaces

Aerial view

Zurich Airport

Airports are among the most characteristic elements of the metropolitan area. They are about to rewrite the geography of the urban territory. In just as similar and emphatic a way as the central station influenced the growth and shape of the city, airports now enhance the economic shift from the main cities towards the urban periphery in metropolitan areas. This shift is the result of improved infrastructural conditions around the airports (major ring roads, public transport corridors and the airports themselves), as compared to other, more central locations.

The surroundings of the airport, and in particular the zones between the airport and the main city centre, are one of the most consistently growing parts of the metropolitan area. The concentration of traffic infrastructures, in some cases bunches of parallel roads and railway lines, gives rise to a new piece of city: the Glattal-Stadt to the north of Zurich, or the E18 logistical corridor in Vantaa, Helsinki. The city of Amsterdam is even undergoing a radical reorientation towards its former southern periphery —nicknamed "the cash corridor"— under the influence of the airport's enormous success. Against the background of such developments, the airport area acquires enormous regional importance.

The increased accessibility of the airport is also attractive for activities other than airport-related ones. As the more advanced airport cities tend to become home to functions that were once monopolised by the city per se, rethinking the role of the airport as a development pole in the metropolitan region becomes an urgent task.

More remote airports like Stockholm Arlanda, Milan Malpensa or London Gatwick, located some 40-60 km from the city, influence their regions in a different way. They are at too great a distance to be viable locations for businesses seeking both proximity to a city

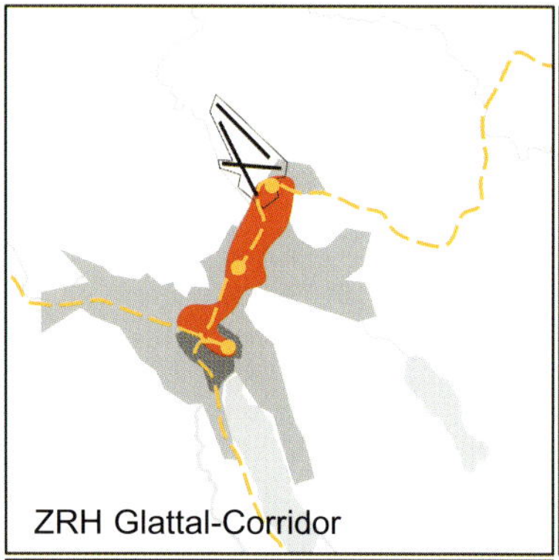

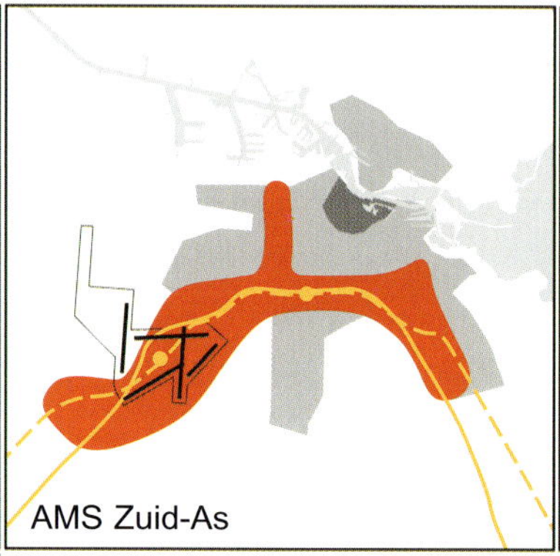

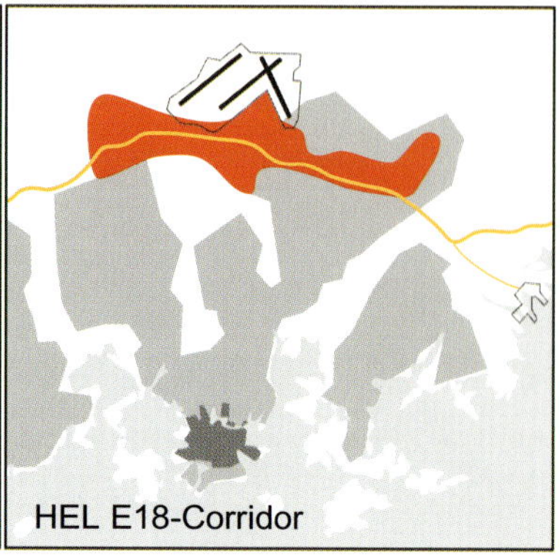

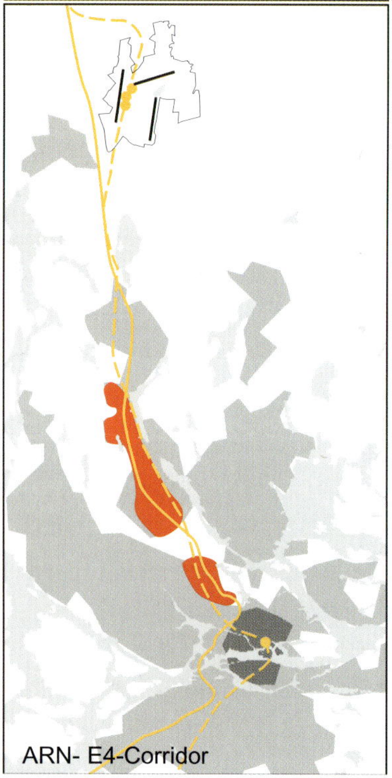

Airports begin to transform the metropolis. Between the centre of the city of ***Zurich*** *and the airport, unprecedented quantities of new urban substance have been built during the last 15 years. The former periphery emerges as one of "the three future cities" of Zurich.*

The ***Amsterdam*** *"Zuid-As" evolves as the number one business location of the Netherlands. It obviously profited from the national "mainport policy" that stimulated growth around Schiphol, defining the airport as both a traffic platform and an economic motor.*

Helsinki *will witness the creation of a major "logistical activity zone" along the third ring road (the E18 TEN route), with an airport city —the Aviapolis— as its showpiece.*

In the Arlanda corridor, north of ***Stockholm****, close to the city centre and with top access to the airport, IT and high-tech businesses settle rapidly.*

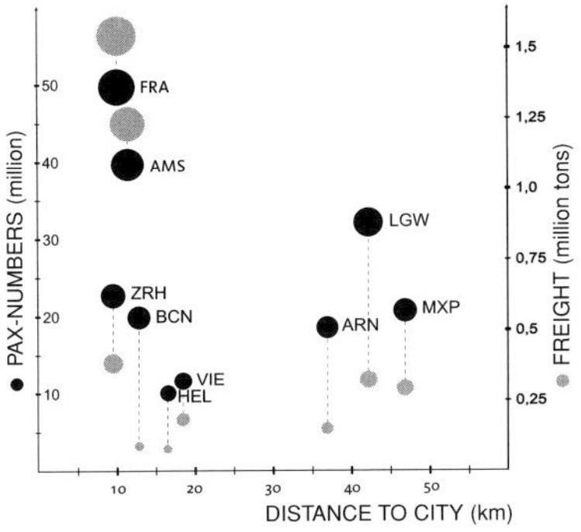

The airport's size and its respective position in the metropolitan area matter. The nearer and bigger it is, the stronger its impact.

and access to air traffic. For such activities, a fast connection to the airport, as provided by the Arlanda-Express, is sufficient. As a consequence, if these airports assume the role of new economic development poles, they will tend, rather, towards specifically airport-related activities, like the North European Logistic Centre in Arlanda. Their impact on the structure of the metropolitan area remains limited.

Polycentric metropolitan areas

Cities are not independent entities any more. They are part of a metropolitan area that may eventually even include several cities, and are thus confronted by new emerging centres. Surrounding municipalities have gained independence due to recent urbanisation processes. Peripheral areas and nearby regional centres have grown much faster than the inner cities have been able to. Proximity to the city centre is becoming relatively less important than a strategic position within the infrastructural networks. This gives rise to highly accessible new centres. The airport is the most prominent of these, and one of the strongest motors of this decentralisation process. In addition, the recent connection of several airport regions to the European HST network —with a stop at the airport and another at the central station— will further enhance the redistribution of centralised activities.

The new dimension and structure of metropolitan areas represents a challenge to traffic planning. Radial relations from, and to, the centre of the main city have become less dominant, while relations between the new regional or metropolitan centres are ever more important. Regional transport initiatives have been launched to respond to these trends, introducing new tangential links across the former periphery.

In many instances such plans aim at better integration of the airport within the metropolitan area. They respond to the fact that some airports already employ the largest daily workforces of the region besides the main city, sometimes involving more than 500 businesses. Outnumbering the biggest companies of the regional economy, and even public administrations, the airport creates its own major housing needs; an ever more critical issue, since the airport surroundings themselves are anything but appropriate to intensive housing. This dilemma has reached alarming proportions at El Prat, Barcelona's airport municipality, which may have to accommodate housing for up to 15,000 employees with the new airport masterplan, instead of the current 3,000.

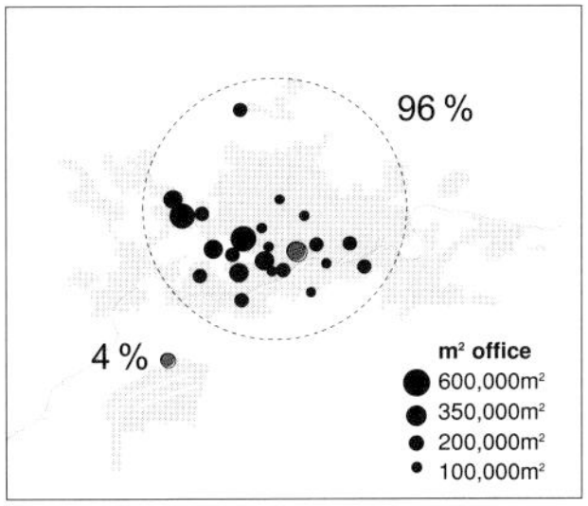

In comparison to other booming centres, current airport cities are not dominant poles in the metropolis in terms of floor space.

The airport against the background of Frankfurt's inner city

The new centrality of airports

Regional spatial planning still lags behind the transformation of the metropolitan area. The "centre versus sub-centres" concept has become outdated. But the shift from plans that define central and peripheral activities to strategies that organise complementarity between the different regional centres has not yet taken place.

As a result, most current policies —especially for major airports— are still dominated by an anxiety about the new centrality of airports. Major developments at the airport are met with suspicion. The concept of an airport city is accompanied by concern on the part of local and regional authorities about the intensive construction activities in and around the airport. It has to be taken into account, however, that on its own an airport city (such as at AMS or FRA) amounts to less than 5% of the total office floor space and future business area in the main cities. It is smaller, then, than other new development hotspots in the region. Also, office projects at the airport mainly compete in a market where the choice is not made between one pole and another in a region, but between different regions as such.

Nevertheless, there is as yet no unanimous agreement on the content of an airport city. To promote the airport anew as an "airport city" seems to have been a publicity stunt on the part of the airport operator aimed at re-qualifying itself in the growing international airport market. The airport operator understands this in global marketing terms, while regional authorities see it in regional planning terms.

Zurich Airport Centre Area

New centres require new policies. Some regions have developed strategies for integrating the airport within the system of regional centres. The crucial questions here are whether airport development is to be limited to functions vital for the operation of an airport, and what the role is it ought to assume with respect to other centres. If the regional initiatives are to be successful, infrastructures and accessibility can no longer lag behind economic strategies. The regional plan for Zurich includes the airport in one of the five regional "Centre Areas". The strategy behind the centre area concept is to concentrate future urban development in the region around the most accessible nodes of public transport. The quality of public transport is perceived as one of the most important factors for overall regional investment.

The centre area policy is a very clear and flexible scheme. The guidelines for it state that "due to the merely partial predictability of urban development dynamics in the region, sites need to be reserved in the centre areas for future use, so as to be able to opti-

The Canton of Zurich declares its airport to be a new "regional centre".

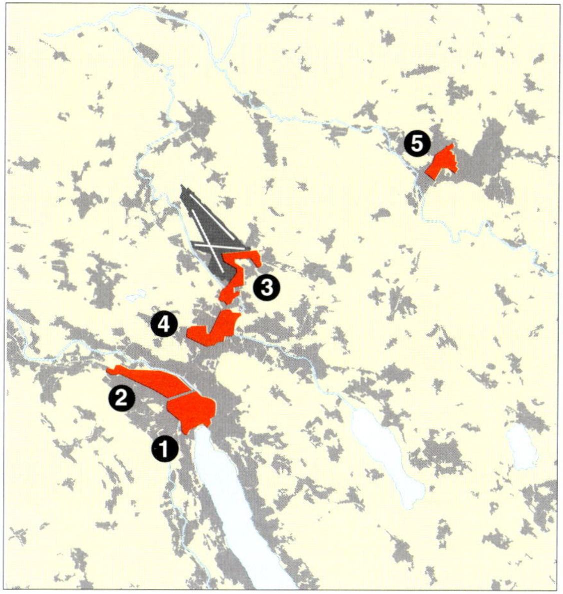

1 Zurich downtown and Central Station area
2 Zurich west urban redevelopment
3 Airport Centre Area
4 Zurich north urban redevelopment
5 Winterthur urban redevelopment

Stockholm County limits Arlanda Airport to becoming an "infrastructural platform". The plan for Greater Stockholm reveals a highly centralised development scheme; regional centre areas are promoted only in densely urbanised areas.

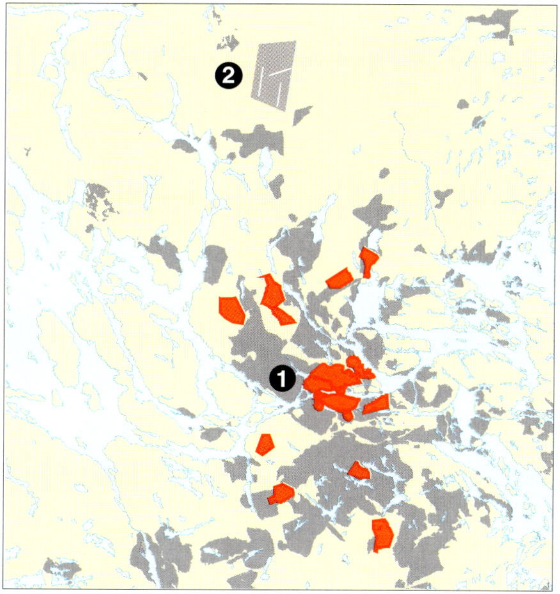

1 Regional centres
2 The airport: "a platform for heavy infrastructure"

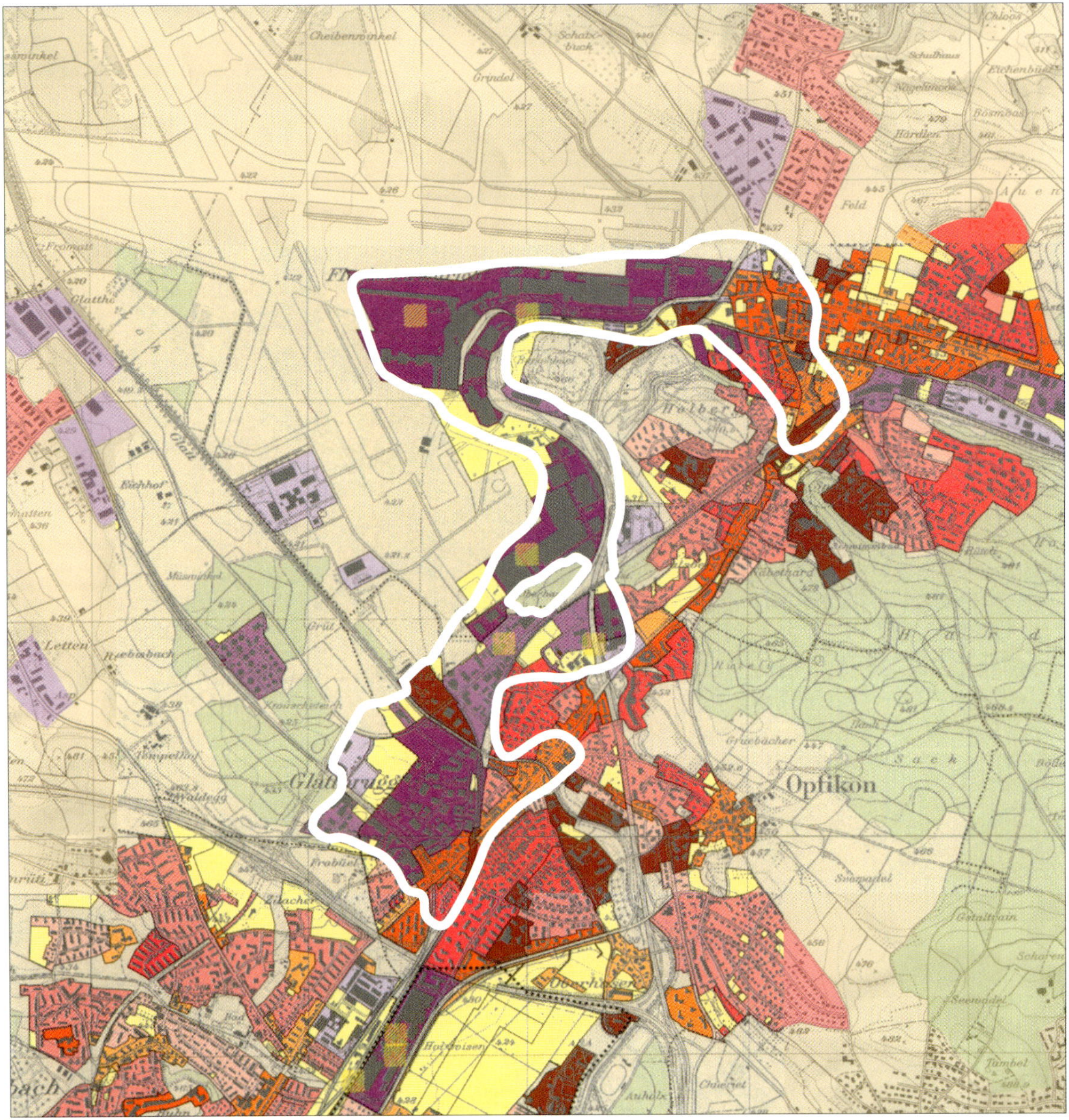

Cheibenwinkel
Grindel
Fromatt
Eichhof
Letten
Tempelhof
Frohbüel
Zilacher
Holberg
Feld
Härdlen
Schulhaus
Chloos
Opfikon
Oberhausen

In Zurich, the airport area is a regional Centre Area. In its guidelines for the concentration of urban development in regional centre areas, the Canton has not been reluctant to include and treat the airport platform in the plan as if it were any other development area. Being only some 5 km long, the Zurich Airport Centre Area contains no less then 4 rail stations, 10 light-rail stops, 3 highway exits, 2 municipal centres and 3 major development sites.

mally accommodate them. [...] Every centre area has to maintain its primary identity, so that they may eventually complement one another. [...] The co-ordination of site development will help in the long term not only to efficiently accommodate, but also to generate, development."This allows, in principle, for fully integrating the airport area in the region, this being treated like other regional development hotspots.

The "airport centre area" has 2.2 million m^2 of built commercial floor area and a development reserve of some 800,000 m^2. The airport itself provides hardly any developable space any more. Hence, the remaining centre area beyond the platform should be carefully developed so as to guarantee the accommodation of airport-related activities. The centre area concept should also help overcome the discrepancy between the immediate real estate demands of the recently privatised airport operator on the one hand, and the availability of highly accessible sites in the wider airport surroundings on the other. Local and regional authority hiccups, like the one caused by relocating the airport operator's headquarters from the terminal area to a remote platform location without adequate accessibility, could thus be avoided.

Most regional strategies, however, are only partially binding. In many instances, regional plans merely have the status of guidelines: these may stimulate investment, but are lacking in actual spatial planning tools. What Zurich and Stockholm have attempted has not yet been achieved in many other regions. There is an inherent lack of correlation between transport planning and land use strategies, due to strictly separated responsibilities within most planning systems: transport and land use planning are split between regional and local authorities respectively.

Space for manoeuvre

Airports are seemingly the manifestation of an incompatible reality: they are attractive location factors, but at the same time they depend on distance. Airports were set up outside the border of cities on green-field sites, just as railway stations were a hundred years ago. Today most airports are not outside, but enmeshed within, the metropolitan area. Even literally remote airports like Gatwick, Arlanda, and especially Malpensa, have been incorporated within fast-growing urban areas that potentially prejudice the airport's future operability. The advantage of the greater availability of land, plus a high degree of accessibility, threaten to become their handicap. Since increased air traffic means that an ever-larger territory will be affected by noise, strategies to keep the city at a distance and guarantee the airport's space for manoeuvre have become urgent. "Zero-development zones" are a highly successful way of limiting the growth of more housing areas. However, they demand a new kind of "anticipatory" planning that goes beyond classical land use planning.

The Dutch government came up with a clever —and finally too costly— scheme for Schiphol Airport, one that made the most of this incompatibility: a downtown terminal with remote runways. It studied the possibility of shifting both the runways and the noise problem to an offshore island, where they would annoy nobody. The terminals were to remain in Schiphol, and the released land around them could have been used for economic development.

As airports become enmeshed, a space for manoeuvre needs to be guaranteed. "Noise contours" or strategic "buffer zones" are deployed to control, restrict and select further urban growth in the vicinity of the airport, and to guarantee long-term open green areas inside the metropolitan area. However, the position and size of the noise contours not only depend on technical factors, but to a great extent on political agreement (Gatwick's "strategic gap").

Amsterdam 1965

Amsterdam 2000

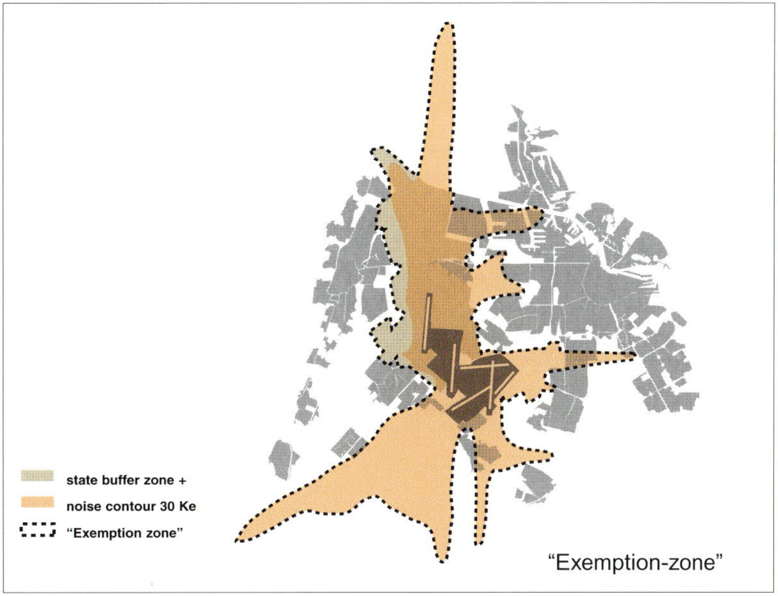
state buffer zone +
noise contour 30 Ke
"Exemption zone"
"Exemption-zone"

2. Airport systems for metropolitan areas

Aerial view

Stockholm Arlanda Airport

In the densely urbanised metropolitan regions of Europe, the expansion of existing airports has reached its limit. Their enmeshing makes it increasingly difficult to satisfy the demand for ever more air traffic. In their current location, extra capacity has to be accommodated within the existing noise contours. Runways under construction in Arlanda, Schiphol and Helsinki are not solely aimed at air traffic growth, but at an improved distribution of noise.

To satisfy the air traffic demands of a larger metropolitan area involves, however, more than simply resolving bottlenecks at the current airport. The extension of a conurbation may actually require an airport system, rather than a bigger single airport.

The goal of an airport system is not so much to establish an operational entity, a "hub airport", in which several airports share the workload. This would require enormous investment in high-speed shuttles to guarantee brief connecting times for transfer passengers. Instead, an airport system has to provide equal access to air traffic for the whole region. On top of that, it has to allow for adequate distribution of the potential benefits. An airport system generally corresponds to a territorial condition different to that of a single central city. Within polycentric metropolitan areas, or within economic macro-regions engulfing several urban centres, airports are becoming the "common property" of several cities and regions. London is at one extreme: a huge metropolis with four airports dotted all around it (and with City Airport at its centre). The Lombardy region, the "heart of the Italian economy", may be at the other extreme: a dispersed, yet densely urbanised, region mainly served today by the international airport of Malpensa at the westernmost edge of the metropolitan area of Milan.

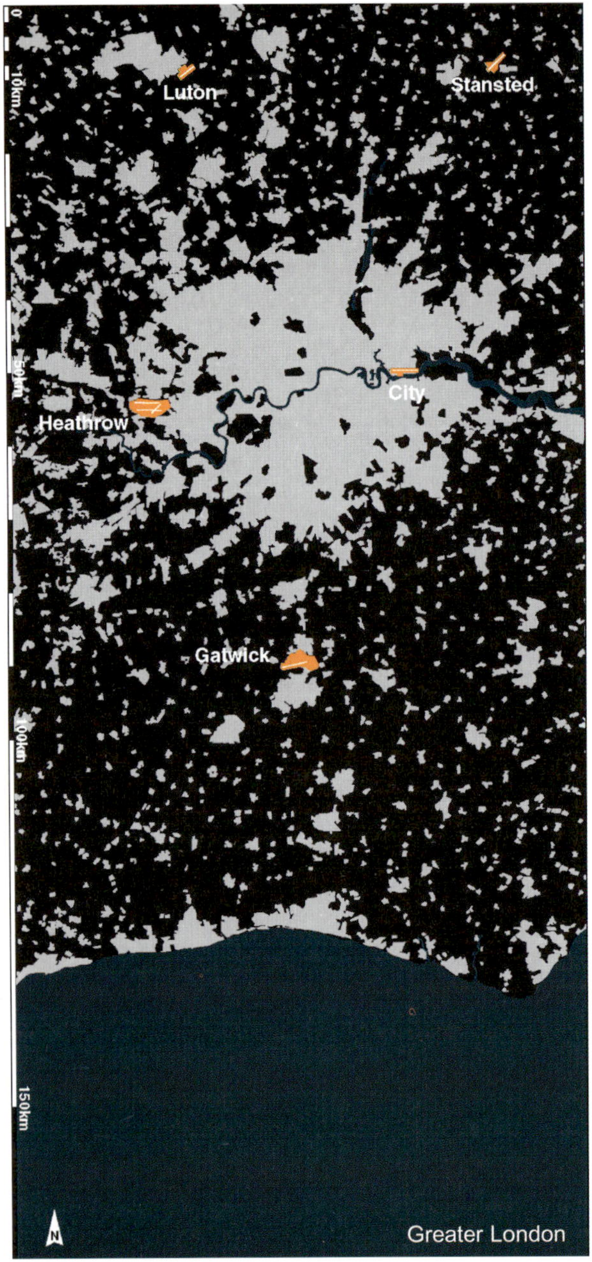

0
10km
50km
100km
150km
Luton
Stansted
City
Heathrow
Gatwick
N
Greater London

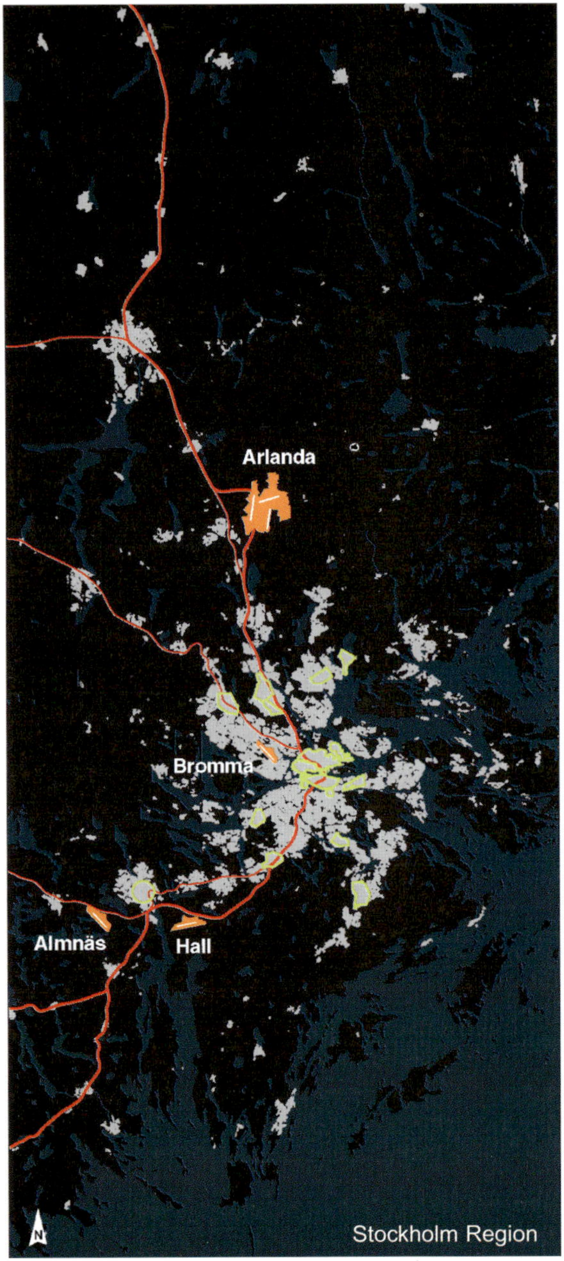

Arlanda
Bromma
Almnäs
Hall
N
Stockholm Region

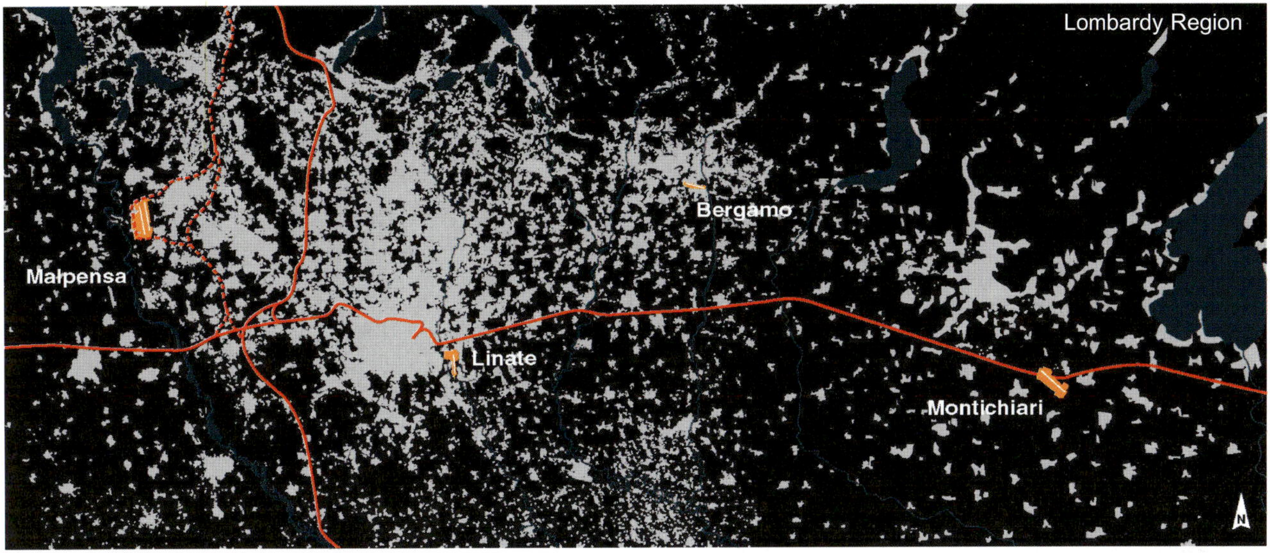
Lombardy Region
Bergamo
Malpensa
Linate
Montichiari

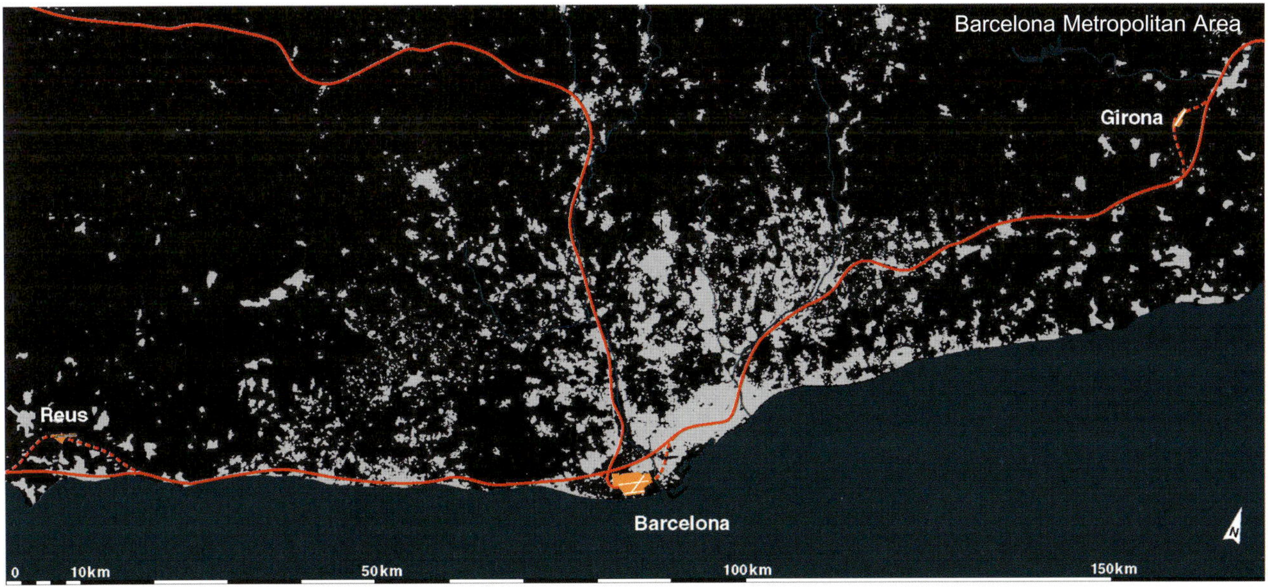
Barcelona Metropolitan Area
Girona
Reus
Barcelona
0
10km
50km
100km
150km

London: the classic airport system

London is a special case. It is served by an airport system of five airports relatively close to the city. Even though often referred to as a single hub of 100 million passengers, the London airport system has hardly any transfer passengers between the various airports. It takes between one and two hours to get from one airport to another. The system actually consists of two fully independent hubs, Heathrow with 56 million and Gatwick with 32 million passengers, and one more airport aspiring to the same status, Stansted. London has grown so big, and has such a congested traffic network, that one single airport, however enormous, would be inadequate. The four outer airports are evenly distributed around London in order to serve all parts of the metropolis.

Previous pages
The diameters of European airport systems —built or planned— are surprisingly similar. They range between 100 to 150km in diameter, a dimension that corresponds to the requirements of the entire metropolitan area.

Barcelona: a system based on the HST?

The idea for a Catalan airport system, including the regional airports of Girona and Reus/Tarragona, has arisen because the growth of Barcelona Airport is, once its current expansion phase is completed, only possible out to sea at prohibitively high costs.

Discussion about connecting the Barcelona metropolitan area to the HST network has been closely linked to the question of how to expand airport capacity. Both the regional and municipal authorities of Barcelona have always assumed a very clear position vis-à-vis the Spanish government about including their airport in the HST network. In terms of a future airport system, a link between all three airports has become crucial. The reason for this is not to connect the airports to each other, but to give the metropolitan area of Barcelona, with its 4 million inhabitants, and cities from Valencia in the south to Toulouse in France, equally excellent and rapid access

A big opportunity presented itself for London to complement its four peripheral airports with the downtown City Airport, which directly served the major redevelopment of the Docklands.

to three complementary airports. In view of these plans, it may be necessary to issue temporary planning and building restrictions, to prevent the rural areas around Girona and Reus Airports from simply filling up.

A north-Italian airport system?

The Lombardy region is considering providing equal access to air traffic at the level of the macro-region. Having reached its current size —20 million passengers— in only two years, Milan Malpensa Airport will have to face capacity constraints sooner than was expected: it does not lie on a green-field site, but within already heavily urbanised surroundings. Perhaps even more crucial is the remote position of Malpensa. It is not the obvious airport choice for a large part of the Greater Milan area and the eastern half of northern Italy. The creation of a Milanese, or even a north-Italian airport system (Venice, Bologna, Bergamo/Brescia, Malpensa), is therefore being evaluated, instead of pursuing the idea of a single major hub at Malpensa.

The preference, today, is to complement Malpensa Airport with a second north-Italian hub, Brescia-Montichiari. This still little-known airstrip is at an acceptable distance from Milan, along the HST line to Venice. Its position in the midst of the major cities of Brescia, Cremona, Mantua and Verona also makes it suitable as a location for certain regional activities —besides air traffic— within this city network. This means that Malpensa might not become the single hub airport for northern Italy that was once envisaged. As a result, its integration within the national and international rail networks —an urgent requirement if it wishes to join the major European hubs— runs the risk of irrelevance: the critical mass of passengers could well be lacking.

A catalyst for the development of south Stockholm?

In Stockholm a new southern airport moved to the forefront of debate about extra airport capacity, not because of constraints at Arlanda Airport —the option of simply expanding this airport would not cause major technical or local problems— but because of the prevailing north-south imbalance in the distribution of development opportunities in the Greater Stockholm region.

Airport-related development and investment is today only triggered in the northern half of Stockholm and in the corridor between Stockholm and Arlanda Airport. An airport to the south would encourage a similar dynamic in, and attract high-value investment to, the southernmost areas of Stockholm. Furthermore, the new airport area would be strongly promoted and form a regional centre zone. It would contribute to increased accessibility between the southern municipalities, and also with downtown Stockholm. Ultimately, the decision has been to concentrate airport expansion at Arlanda Airport itself —not only for environmental reasons, but also because of the concern on the part of the neighbouring counties in the south that a new airport would compete with their own (community-owned or private) airports.

3. A new airport image

Aerial view

Amsterdam-Schiphol Airport

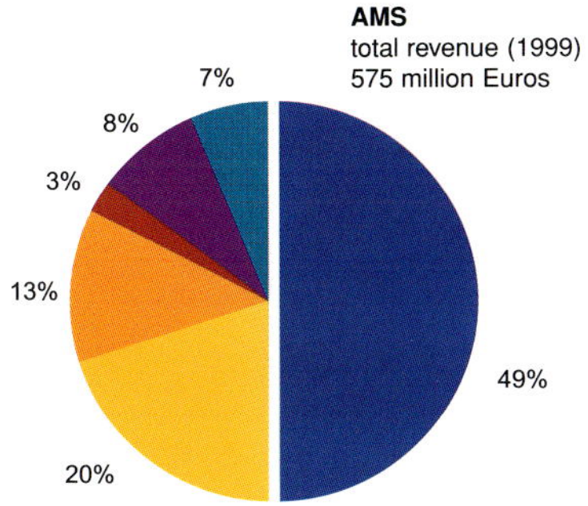

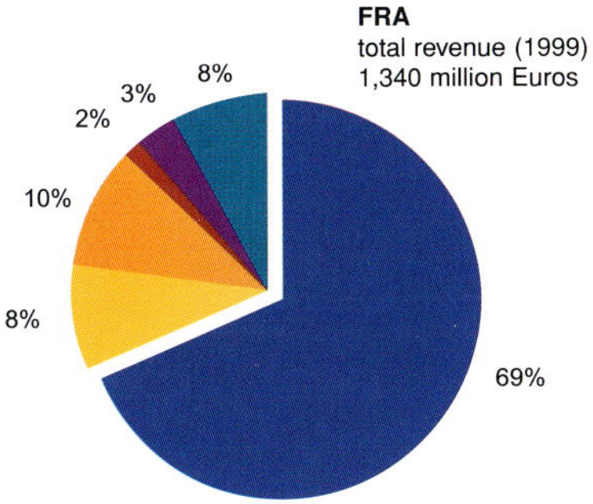

Aviation

Non-aviation
Concessions
Real estate
Services
Parking
Other activities

Non-aviation revenues (e.g. commercial activities) are increasingly important for airports. At London-Heathrow, Paris-Charles de Gaulle or Amsterdam-Schiphol Airports, they have become good for up to 50% of the airport's profits. Frankfurt has a much larger total turnover than Schiphol, because it provides most ground services for airlines by itself. Schiphol gives corresponding concessions to service providers.

Airport operators have launched a new "airport image". It no longer relies on high-tech terminal architecture, runway capacity or passenger comfort alone. Two recent trends have become essential to this new image. On the one hand, the airport promotes AiRail intermodality. Improving the transfer between air and rail increases the airport's competitiveness. Investment by airport and rail operators in the quality of the airport station, and also in efficient bus services to and from the airport, have become crucial to accommodating further growth.

On the other hand, airport operators are urged to assume a new —and more commercial— business outlook that goes far beyond mere aviation concerns. Airport operators can no longer rely on state subsidies. The narrow profits made by the aviation business no longer suffice for the increasing investment needed to expand and maintain the airport infrastructure. Forced to optimise their income, airports increasingly seek to cash in on landside development, real estate and concessions; in short, additional revenue from non-aviation activities. Promoting this commercial reality, the airport proposes that meeting, doing business and shopping could all be carried out there. Once a mere airfield with a terminal, the "airport product" becomes much more complex today. The airport city is part of the comprehensive task of running an airport.

Exporting a brand image

The "new airport image" is also the "new airport brand". Airport operators no longer limit their activities to their airport location alone. They aim at exporting their specific "airport brand", and getting involved in airport and airport city development abroad. There, around the world, some two hundred airport projects are in the

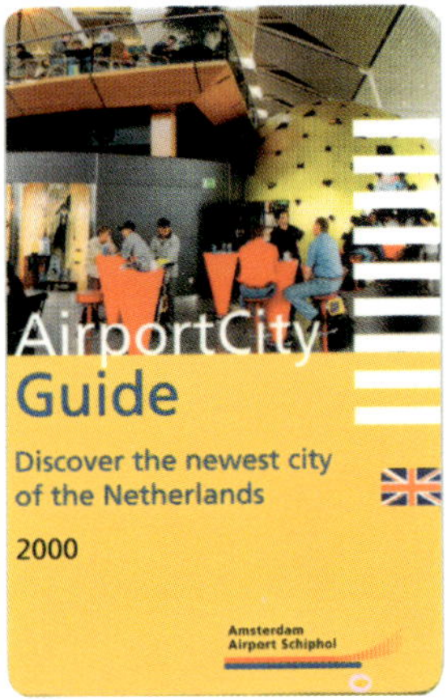

AMS

ARN

BCN

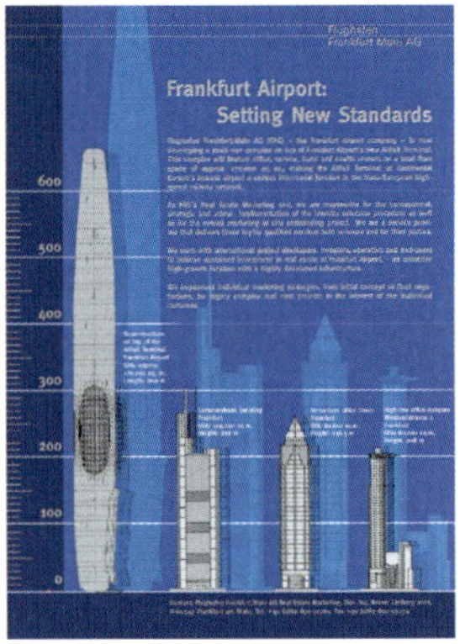

FRA

LGW

HEL

MXP

VIE

ZRH

pipeline for the next five years, thirty of them being major projects in "strategic markets". This perspective exceeds the opportunities at the established operator's home base. Privatisation is considered essential by airport operators, so as to be able to participate in this global market. Independence from state capital, along with entrepreneurial management, is a prerequisite.

Airport alliances

In order to strengthen their international position, airports have begun to form airport alliances. In 1999 Frankfurt and Schiphol Airports established a new co-operation deal called "Pantares". This joint venture aims at increasing the airports' cash flow by combining their specific expertise in airport development in other countries; namely real estate developments and shopping concepts, transfer of know-how and IT services. However, in the light of this co-operation there may also be issues of airport city development at the two airports themselves. The prospect of such international airport alliances will eventually expand the range of players and introduce counterparts to airport regions which are less familiar and have no ties with the local context.

The image discloses ambitions. Intermodality and business orientations appear in different graduations in the slogans of different airports. While some still stress their quality as an airfield, others shift the emphasis to a combination of air traffic, intermodality and real estate development, and ultimately to a new "airport product", an airport city.

Reorganisation of the Airport Authority

Such an extensive range of activities means that airport operators forego the status of being a mere "transport operator". The new strategies involved lead to a radical reorganisation of the company structure. Around the core business of airport operation —which publishes the classic "annual report"— new business departments evolve:

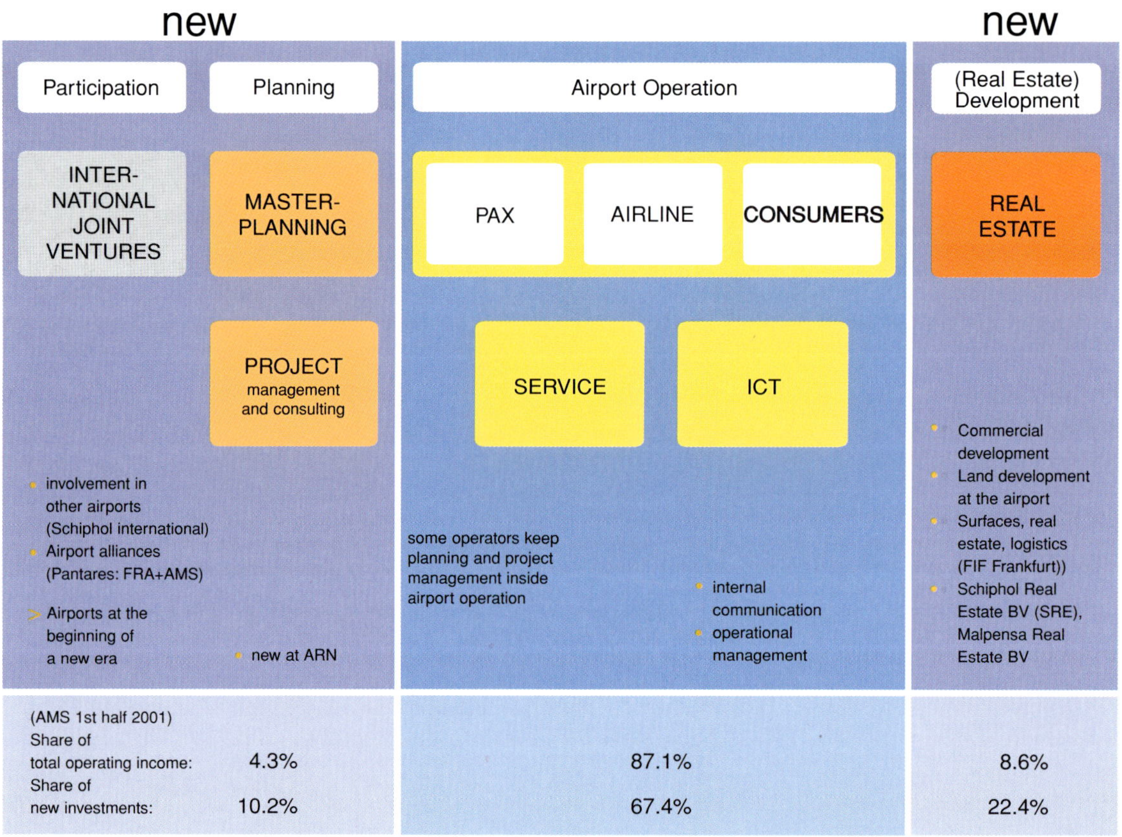
new
new
Participation
Planning
Airport Operation
(Real Estate) Development
INTER-NATIONAL JOINT VENTURES
MASTER-PLANNING
PAX
AIRLINE
CONSUMERS
REAL ESTATE
PROJECT management and consulting
SERVICE
ICT
involvement in other airports (Schiphol international)
Airport alliances (Pantares: FRA+AMS)
Airports at the beginning of a new era
new at ARN
some operators keep planning and project management inside airport operation
internal communication
operational management
Commercial development
Land development at the airport
Surfaces, real estate, logistics (FIF Frankfurt))
Schiphol Real Estate BV (SRE), Malpensa Real Estate BV
(AMS 1st half 2001)
Share of total operating income:
4.3%
87.1%
8.6%
Share of new investments:
10.2%
67.4%
22.4%

By establishing new business branches, airports become ever more market-oriented enterprises. They not only "operate" but also "develop" the airport platform and prepare for participation in the international airport market.

- master-planning department, for controlling the organisation of the territory;
- real estate branch: their own land use and real estate development company, which now edits own publications (like SRE's *Building at Airports 1995-2000*);
- an international affairs bureau, for claiming a share in the global airport development market.

The organisation of an airport begins to look like the structure of a local authority: fulfilling a public duty (facilitating air traffic), and at the same time providing the basic conditions for developing the territory. Such a reorganisation of the airport operator is not limited to a certain type of airport ownership. It applies to public-owned enterprises (AMS, BCN, MXP), just as it does to (partly) privatised airport operators (FRA, VIE, ZRH), and even to state operators (ARN). New ideas are introduced by new people; or, put the other way —as is the case with BAA— no change to the management team means that the business outlook stays pretty much the same.

Often, though, the old and new departments are somewhat split, due to differing management cultures: airside planning, the core competence, is still rather conservative, while the new business departments are very market-oriented.

Responsibilities

In order to assume both the role of a real estate developer and public transport operator, a major change in the philosophy of airport operation is required. With privatisation, straightforward entrepreneurial reasoning becomes the norm, and replaces "public" management. Running an airport now means developing and operating its landside infrastructure too, along with a complete package of companies and services present around an airport. A "total concept" is needed to balance airside and airport city development.

Not surprisingly, the airport attempts to shift its power as a planning authority from the airside to its new business activities on the landside. This shift brings implicit conflicts with local and regional authorities in its wake. Two questions are particularly preoccupying: should it be the airport operator's exclusive domain not only to run the airport, but also to develop real estate at this major regional and international interchange node? And if not, how are the responsibilities to be reassigned between airport and local/regional authorities with respect to the new activities of the airport?

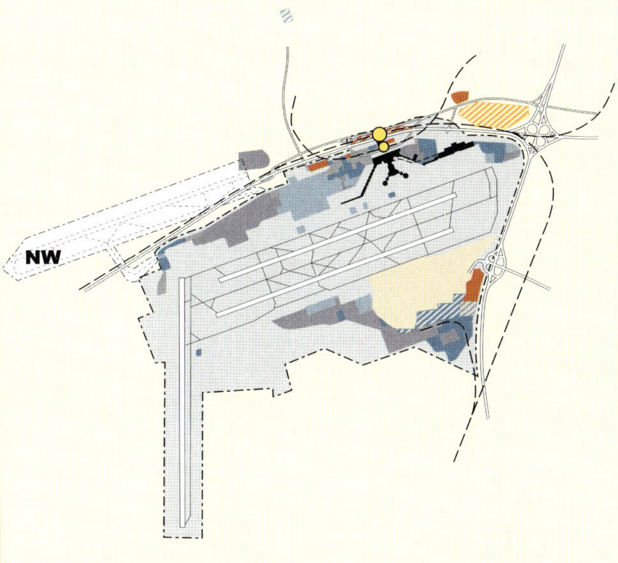

FRA

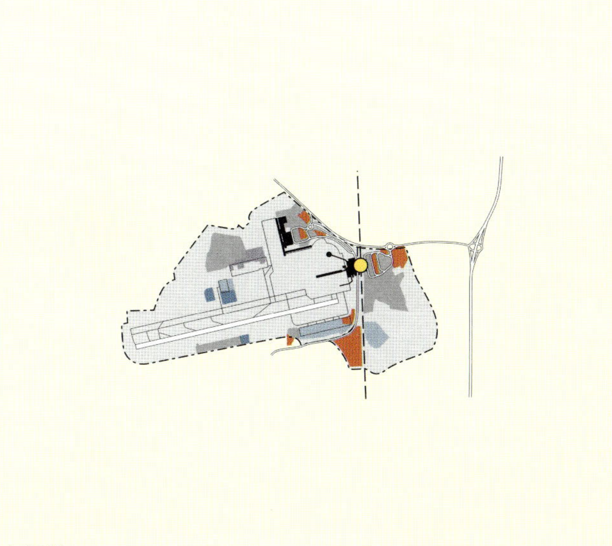

LGW

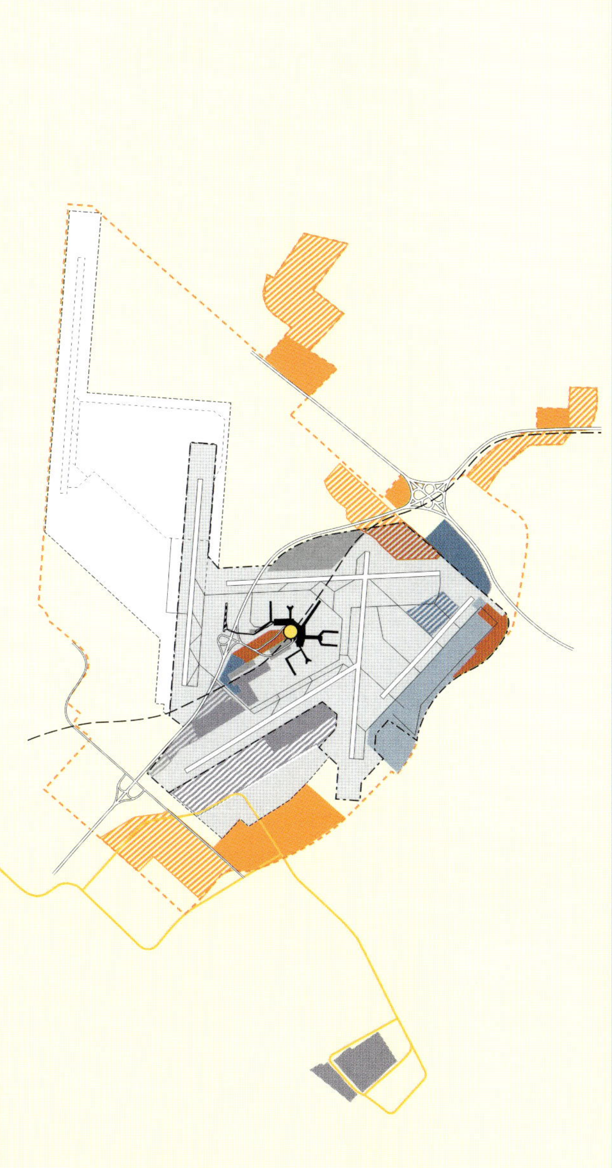

AMS

ZRH
MXP
BARCELONA SEAPORT
BCN
Aircraft maintenance
Airport support services
Freight
Terminal areas
Tertiary activities
Logistics
Planned areas
Parking
Reserve
Airport interchange node
Airport perimeter
0
5Km
10Km

ARN

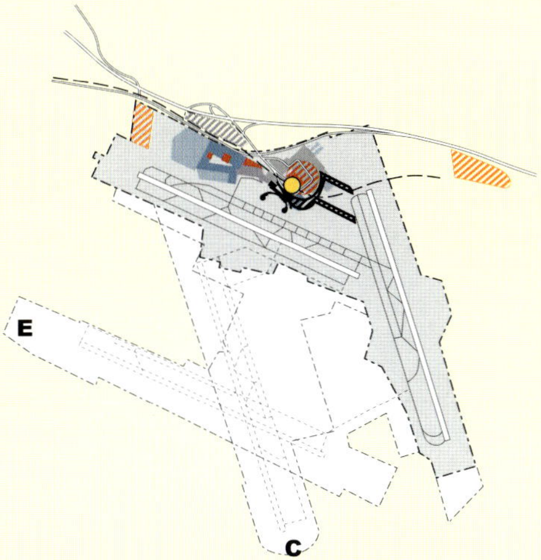

VIE (main alternatives)

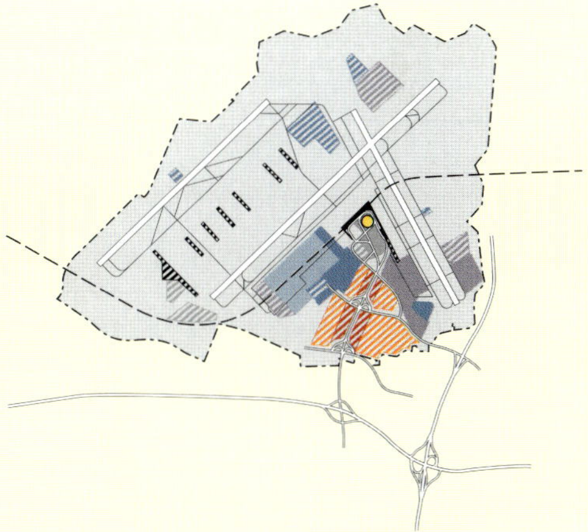

HEL

4. From airport to airport city

Aerial view

Helsinki Vantaa Airport

Renewing the airport

Airports have always changed very fast. They have been constantly redesigned, with runways being added or terminals extended to provide additional gates. The extraordinary rise in air traffic over the last decade has initiated further renovation of the airport world-wide, but this time the renewal is more radical than before. There is an obvious need to reserve space for airside and operational activities —the core business of the airport. Flexibility as to future expansion of the airport machinery itself is crucial, in order to anticipate the still-huge forecasts of increasing volumes of cargo and passenger traffic.

The latest generation of expansion plans is stimulated not only by the need for more asphalt or gates, however: it involves the landside layout of the airport territory at least as much as the airside facilities. Alongside the operator's new business strategies, there is a wish to provide locations close to the airport centre for non-aviation activities that bring much-needed extra revenue for running a contemporary airport.

In addition, airport operators —like port authorities— wish not only to handle freight, but also to add value to the growing volumes of freight flows. "Cargo cities" —compact compounds of logistic and light-industrial activities on the platform itself— become increasingly common, and they invade every corner of the airport's territory, however remote. Exploiting airfreight seems especially attractive if there is an opportunity to combine this with the freight flows of a seaport, as in Barcelona, or in conjunction with already established distribution centres and logistic terminals, such as the rail yards near Malpensa Airport.

Elasticity

Gatwick, Europe's number five in passenger traffic terms, has the smallest platform, with 674 ha. Arlanda Airport, medium-sized in terms of passenger numbers, is a giant with 3,000 ha. There is no direct correlation, then, between passenger numbers or tons of freight handled and the size of the airport platform. Also, the size of the platform does not reveal the business orientation of airport operators —bigger does not mean more airport city. Airport perimeters were not conceived to accommodate major landside developments but, in the first instance, to guarantee operation and future capacity expansion.

With the next round of renovation, the size of the perimeter starts to be measured not only in terms of the elasticity required for the operation and optimal performance of an airport, but also in terms of the ambition to accommodate extra business and commercial development. An increasingly diverse mix of activities competes for space and a privileged sites on the platform —the territory "governed" by the airport operator. This challenges former functional hierarchies in platform organisation. The terrain of spatial layout is shifting.

Particularly large airports located close to, or within, urbanised areas are presented with a dilemma. Development pressure on their land is exacerbated, since they are subject to two seemingly incompatible factors: their size means high air traffic growth in absolute numbers, while at the same time they are the prime candidates for a most successful airport city development, due to their proximity to the city. And in order not to be suffocated by their own economic success in the long-term, airports are forced to devise strategies for maintaining space to manoeuvre —a complicated balancing act. The setting aside of airport territory has to be made in order to

There is no direct relationship between the scale of operations and the size of the platform.

The airport centre: once a parking field (AMS 1977)...

...now a valuable resource for more prestigious activities (AMS 1998).

guarantee the flexible development of airport infrastructures in the future. This flexibility, however, is already severely restricted due to the increasing constraints imposed by the city closing in on the airport: parameters for runway layout and flight management are no longer free, but dictated by the surrounding urbanisation.

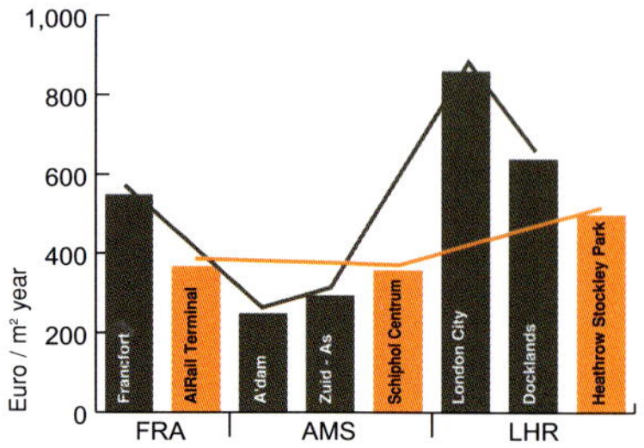

Real estate rentals on European airports are similar, but differ radically in the central areas of cities.

A switching of positions

Obliged to resolve the contradictory claims on their limited land, airports set out to use their territory more efficiently. The trick is to creatively maximise the value of scarce and contested land. Freight handling needs, plane maintenance, catering and parking facilities are weighed against the demands for more hotels, conference and business facilities. A new distribution or redistribution of activities on the platform seems inevitable. A balance has to be found between functions that need to be there, and others that, being willing to pay, are profitable for the operator.

At airports with a rapid growth in air traffic and in non-aviation activities, this leads to a "switching of positions" within the airport perimeter. At Frankfurt, Schiphol, Vienna and Zurich Airports —all relatively close to the city— the positions near the interchange, and thus close to the terminals, are becoming too valuable for mere parking and freight-handling purposes. These activities are removed step by step from the core to make way for a new field of airport operation: the realisation of non-aviation activities.

For land close to the terminals, prime site prices are paid, comparable or superior to the best locations in the nearby city: 350 Euros per m² for AMS and FRA. Not only is profitable, short-term parking being stacked on various levels (a sign of rising land prices), even building on top of infrastructures and terminals is no longer the exception. The 170,000 m² of commercial space on a single platform

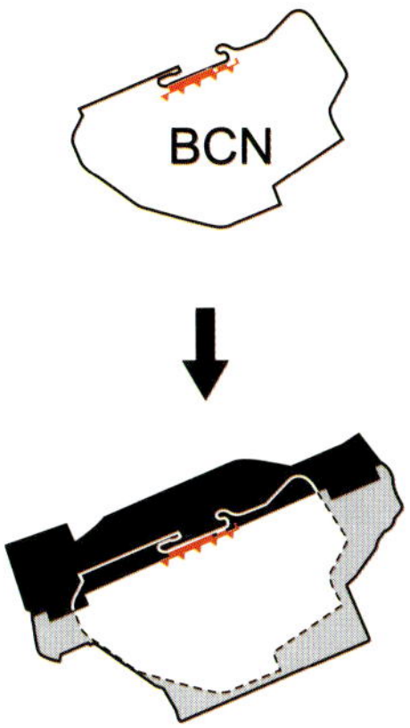

Barcelona will nearly double its platform size with the expansion of the airport.

above the AiRail terminal in Frankfurt is probably the example of most "intensive land use" at an airport right now. Until recently, such enormous pre-investments were only thinkable downtown, at the central station.

Rotation on the airport platform not only affects its central location. Positions are reshuffled even at the periphery. Schiphol, for example, plans its new business parks on former remote parking areas and on the former Fokker Industries site.

Expansion?

At most airports, though, the switching of positions and intensification of land use on the platforms has become insufficient. Even the organisation of apparently generous sites turns out to be hopelessly inadequate in face of the double-digit growth in air traffic and the growing attractiveness of airports as business locations. The airport perimeter becomes ever more restricted.

As new runways are being planned or built (when they still fit into the restricted spatial conditions), airport operators view the necessary enlargement of their territory as a chance to acquire control over more land for other, non-aviation activities. AENA negotiated a perimeter expansion for Barcelona Airport that encompasses generous new spaces for its logistical and commercial programme, and allows for planning a compact airport city from scratch.

But since the growth of airside capacity is already controversial enough, most local authorities want to strictly limit expansion of the perimeter to operational activities, or they even require trade-offs, with land from the former perimeter reverting to them. In order to gain additional space in crucial positions on their platform, airports are therefore obliged to apply other strategies.

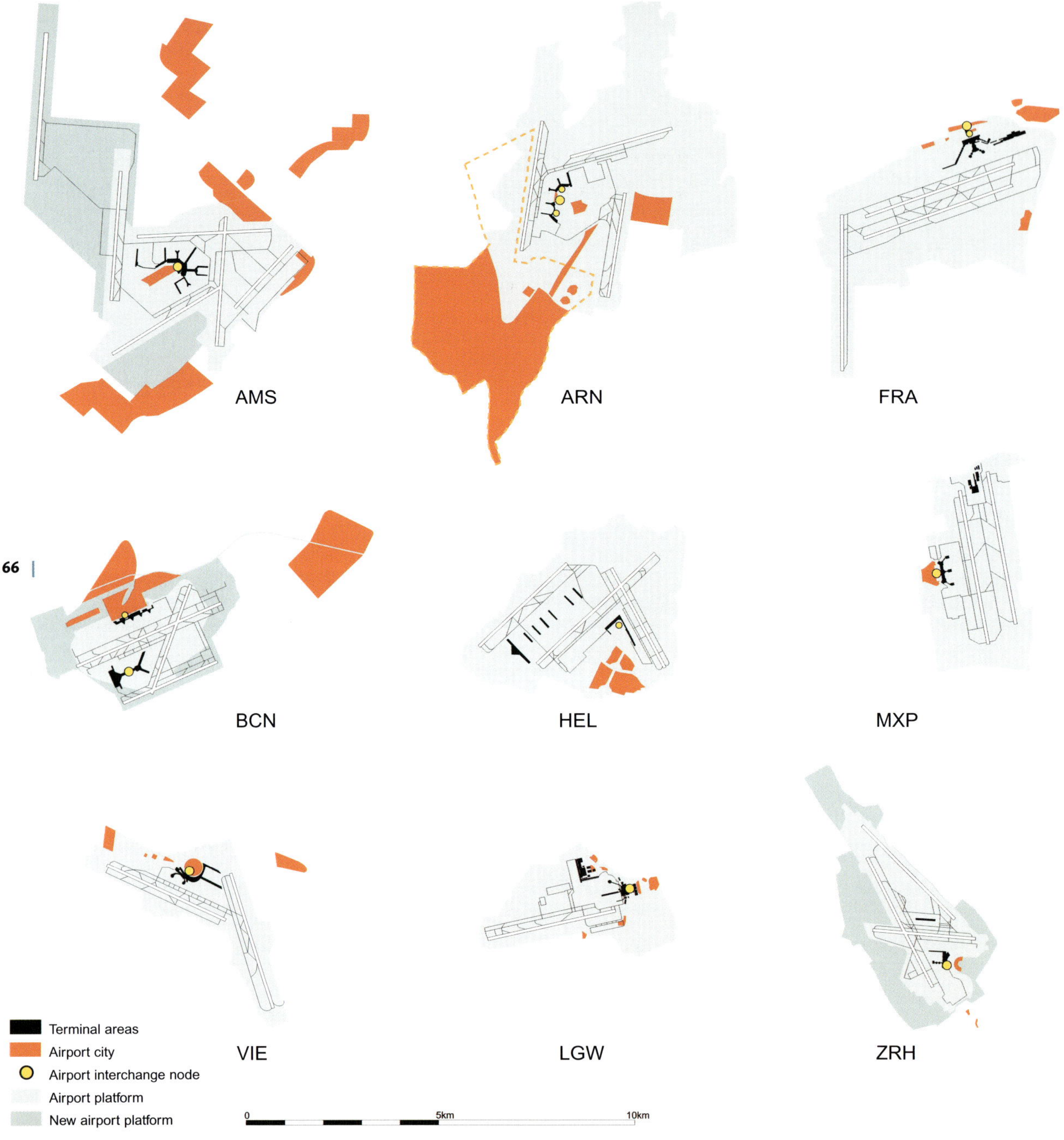
AMS
ARN
FRA
BCN
HEL
MXP
VIE
LGW
ZRH
Terminal areas
Airport city
Airport interchange node
Airport platform
New airport platform
0
5km
10km

Patterns and dimensions of airport cities: on top of the interchange (ARN and FRA); spread across the territory (AMS and LGW); a compact airport city (HEL, MXP and VIE); a designated logistical area (ARN and BCN).

Outsourcing

Parts of the core business such as long-term parking, freight handling or catering, can be relocated to the surroundings of the platform, as long as they remain well connected to the core of the airport. This may require major infrastructural investment: Schiphol connects future remote cargo areas that are way beyond its own territory, next to the globally operating flower fair, by means of an automated 5-km-long underground logistical system (ULS) to the platform and to a new AiRail service centre for freight.

Joint ventures

To guarantee space for airport-related activities in the vicinity of the airport, activities that are crucial to the competitiveness of their air freight operations, airport operators need to co-operate with the authorities beyond their own perimeter. In Amsterdam, for instance, they co-operate, via the Schiphol Area Development Company (SADC), in the development of specific airport-related activities (mostly logistical activities) in the immediate vicinity of the airport.

Urban standards

In spite of, or more often due to, these varied attempts to overcome spatial constraints, the airport platform becomes increasingly complex. Often, the lack of space does not permit a compact set of facilities and an airport city. Constant reorganisation of the airport in order to satisfy ever more diverse demands leads to a fragmented platform layout, one at odds with the new airport image. FRA set up facilities both to the north and to south of the runways; AMS and

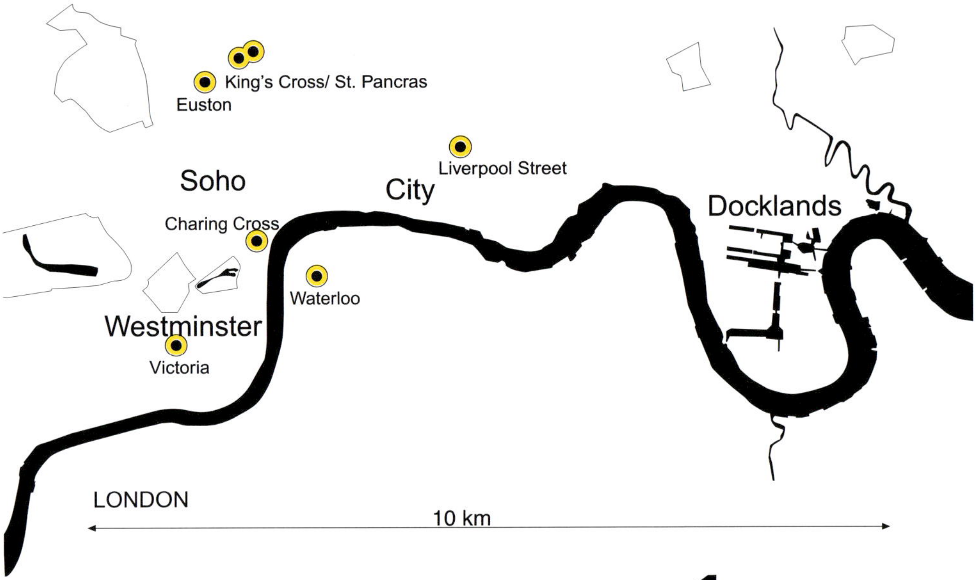

LONDON

FRA

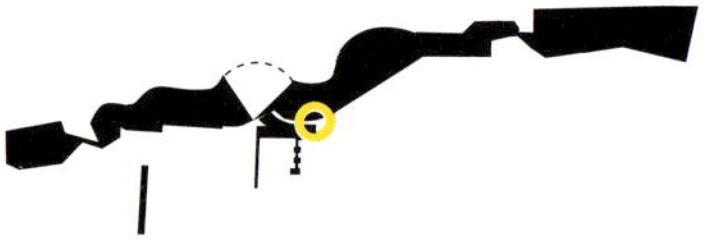

ZRH

LGW

Dispersed non-operational areas make access difficult.
Wrapped around the runways, distances between airside facilities may seem rather short. On their landside, however, airport platforms become increasingly complex. They turn into many-km-long accumulations of a manifold spectrum of activities. Can the airport's accessibility still rely on one airport station only?

LGW feature facilities all around the outside of their perimeters. Freight handling, maintenance, catering, business parks, logistical centres and remote parking are so dispersed that efficient internal means of transport have to be developed to keep the airport territory functioning.

For such patchwork-like layouts, classic airport expansion plans will no longer suffice. Airport planning has an established tradition of infrastructural planning focussed on airside and landside traffic flows. This is best reflected in the concentration on road access, something that has usually made the landside layout resemble an inscrutable jumble of access roads and parking lots.

The question arises as to whether, given the increasing importance of the airport infrastructure and the aim of creating airport cities, the sphere of action of airport planning need not be defined much more broadly: altered business strategies have radically modified the condition of the airport. The image of the airport needs a facelift in order to be successful in presenting the new airport product. In that respect, and in order to overcome a merely functional set-up and to create a degree of quality for the surroundings too, some airport operators have begun to apply the tools of urban planning to their territory.

This facelift is, however, usually not left to the discretion of the airport operators alone. In most instances the public authorities question such a wide portfolio of activities, activities which often include strategic land use and real estate management. They emphasise the fact that running an airport is a concession and not just a business or public administrative function, and insist on clearly distinguishing operational and non-operational activities on the platform.

Airport City

An airport city is, above all, a business strategy on the part of the airport operator, aimed at cashing in on the business opportunities created by its operations and the important function it provides in landside transport networks. Operators use it as a label for indicating their new business outlook: they are not only facilitating air traffic, but are also offering commercial services.

An airport city also involves regional development. An airport city does not stand alone. It is not detached from the airport surroundings, but is part of a broader regional strategy that orients itself towards the landside traffic function of the airport, and intends to take advantage of the spin-offs from the airport.

In terms of territorial definition, the airport city is, in principle, the more or less dense cluster of operational, airport-related activities, plus other commercial and business concerns, on and around the airport platform. However, this cluster is called an airport city only if it shows the qualitative features of a city (density, access quality, environment, services).

The term "Airport City" has also been used differently. When it first appeared in the USA in the 1970s, it tended to mean industrial and business parks right next to an airfield. In Helsinki, the airport municipality uses the term for itself: "Vantaa, the Airport City".

Arlanda's Skycity, conceived as a hinge between terminals, and located right on top of the rail station, provides 80,000m² of hotels, congress lounges, restaurants and business premises.

HEL: Aviapolis

As yet there are very few local authorities that actively involve themselves in establishing criteria for the quality of airport city developments.

In Finland airports are classified as “traffic zones” within local zoning, and designated for transport purposes only. Accordingly, in Helsinki planning of the airport infrastructure and support facilities is assigned to the state-owned CAA, overruling municipal control over land use planning. At the same time, though, the CAA also obliges the airport to build for transport purposes alone. Areas for non-operational activities, while still belonging to the state, are rezoned and automatically come under the planning authority of the municipality of Vantaa.

This was also the case when the CAA was able —with the perimeter expansion required for a new runway— to free land at the southern entrance of the airport for building an airport city. “Aviapolis”, as it is called, is now a joint initiative of the CAA and Vantaa, and is promoted by both parties. As of now, the respective responsibilities and the distribution of construction costs and benefits are being negotiated between the development partners. In any event, in order to set high standards for the image of the future “Aviapolis” the city of Vantaa has developed a detailed urban plan.

Comparable in a way to Vantaa, the El Prat airport municipality in Barcelona claims planning authority over the non-operational parts of the airport city, the goal being to control the quality of the whole future airport city development. These two cases reveal that it is more than likely that the most successful airport cities will be jointly conceived by airport operators and local/regional authorities.

Official slogan of the City of Vantaa.

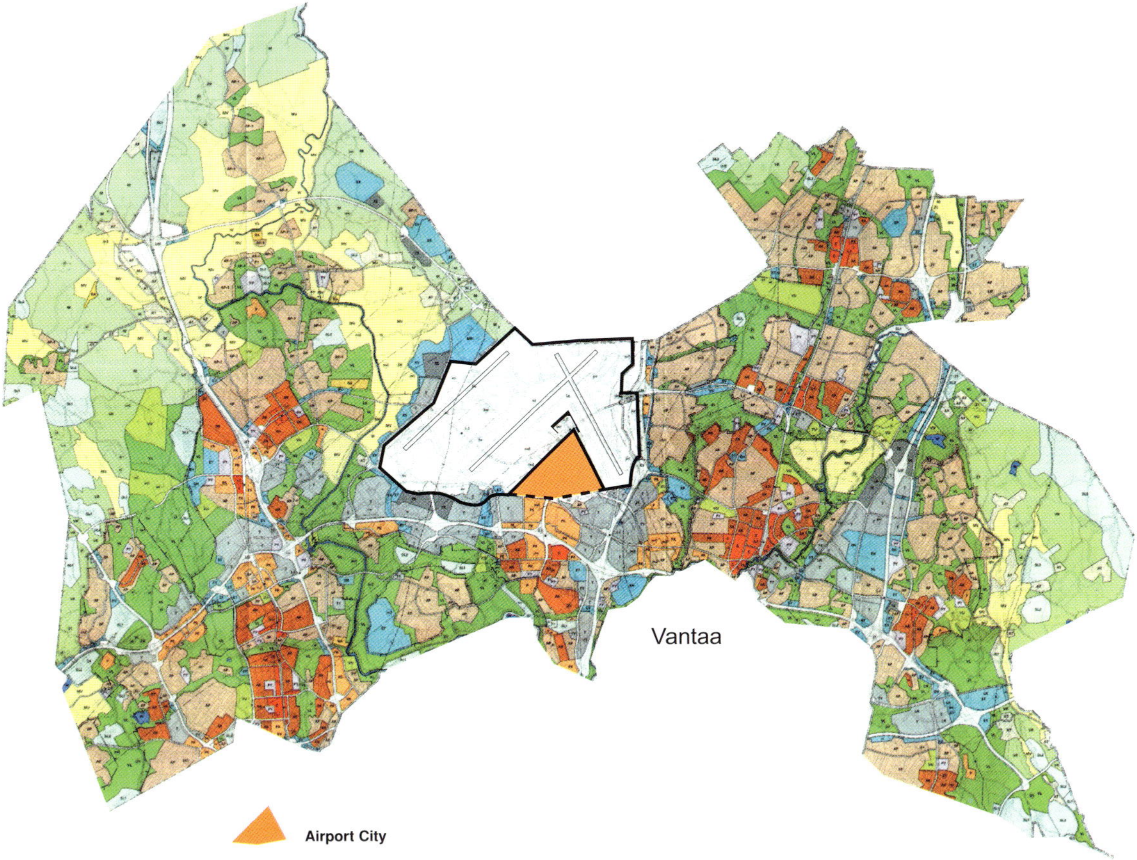

The airport in Vantaa: a white gap in the municipality's land use plan, governed by the CAA Finland.
The new Aviapolis (orange triangle) will be taken out of the "traffic zone". It is subject to the municipality's planning authority, as it concerns the development of non-aviation activities. The 400,000 m² of office, high-tech and IT space and logistical activities are developed by the airport operator and municipality together.

5. Light rail and “Fastway”

Aerial view

London Gatwick Airport

The prospect for rapid and attractive real estate development close to an airport, turning it into one of the top multi-modal interchange nodes in a region, is self-evident. Yet there is a discrepancy between the status which development sites bearing the airport label have, and their quality of access by public transport in general. Even though physically close to the core of the airport, many of these sites lack adequate public transport access, as measured by the standards applied in other urban areas.

Major workforce centres

Platforms become increasingly fragmented and difficult of access. This situation is even more unsatisfactory since airports in general, and the new business activities in particular, generate an enormous number of job opportunities. Airports that grow beyond 20 million passengers become major regional work centres with long work cycles (often 24-hour service economies). They feature between 500 (BCN) and 1,400 (AMS) workplaces per million passengers per annum. With 50,000 and 60,000 employees respectively on their platform, AMS or FRA Airports are by far the biggest workforce concentrations in the region besides the main city; bigger even than jewels of the new economy, like Microsoft with 40,000 employees world-wide, and of the old economy, like Toyota with 65,000. This is an enormous logistical challenge. In absolute numbers, the amount of employees continues to grow. At hubs in particular, where the share of transfer passengers increases, daily employees' trips to and from the airport begin to outnumber the trips generated by passengers.

More than just getting to the airport

The public transport initiatives of airport operators (AMS, LGW), and regional plans to integrate the airport within metropolitan networks (BCN, ZRH).

Access to the airport city calls for something more than access to its terminals alone. Landside accessibility at the airport is very high at the interchange node itself, but is far below "urban" standards over the rest of the territory. If public transport initiatives are limited to AiRail interchange alone, more than 50% of the traffic movements to and from the airport —that is, those movements not generated by air passengers— will be disregarded. The interchange has to be complemented by adequate public transport distribution to the airport city as a whole. The enormous number of workplaces, spread across a vast surface that is often several km^2 large and many kilometres long, the dispersed facilities, and the new development areas all call for an overall traffic management plan for this "small city".

The possibilities for extending existing on-airport people transport systems (people movers) from the terminal area to the dispersed and remote platform areas are being studied. Frankfurt is looking at the elongation of its "SkyLine" people mover system to its southern facilities. These systems usually provide an optimal link to the airport railway station.

More interesting and far-reaching are ambitions to integrate airport platforms within the regional or urban networks more successfully. While traditional dedicated links to the central station in the city predominantly serve air passengers, these new regional public transport lines are planned to guarantee high-access quality in the airport city as a whole. These new connections will provide several stops on the airport territory and in the adjacent business parks: the Zuid-Tangent Amsterdam (7 stops), Linea 9 Barcelona (3 stops planned, 2 more under discussion), Stadtbahn Glattal Zurich (6-8 stops planned).

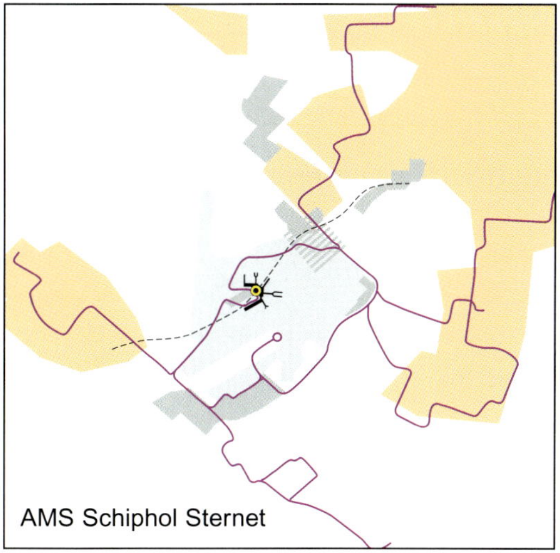
AMS Schiphol Sternet

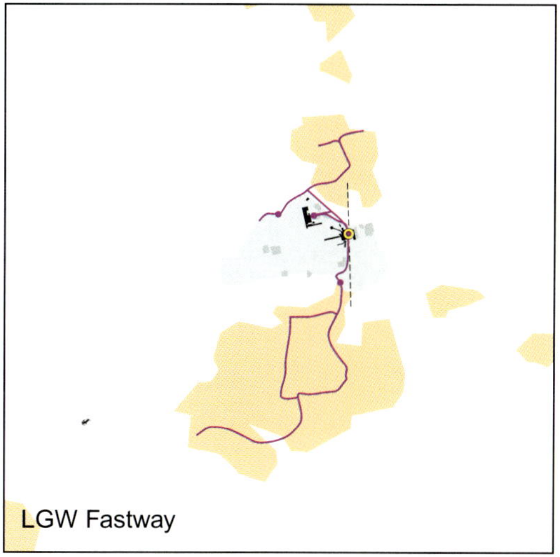
LGW Fastway

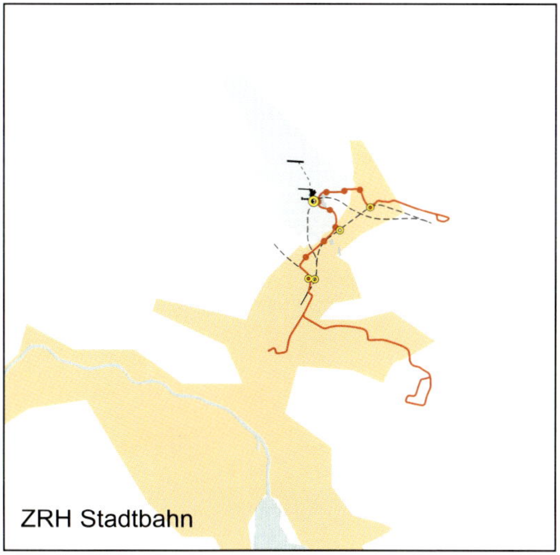
ZRH Stadtbahn

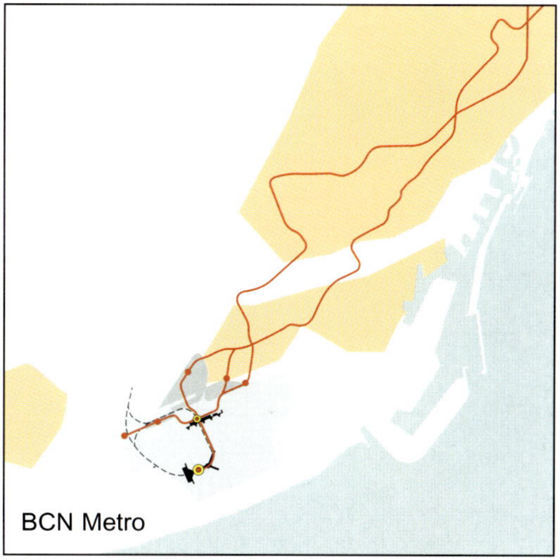
BCN Metro

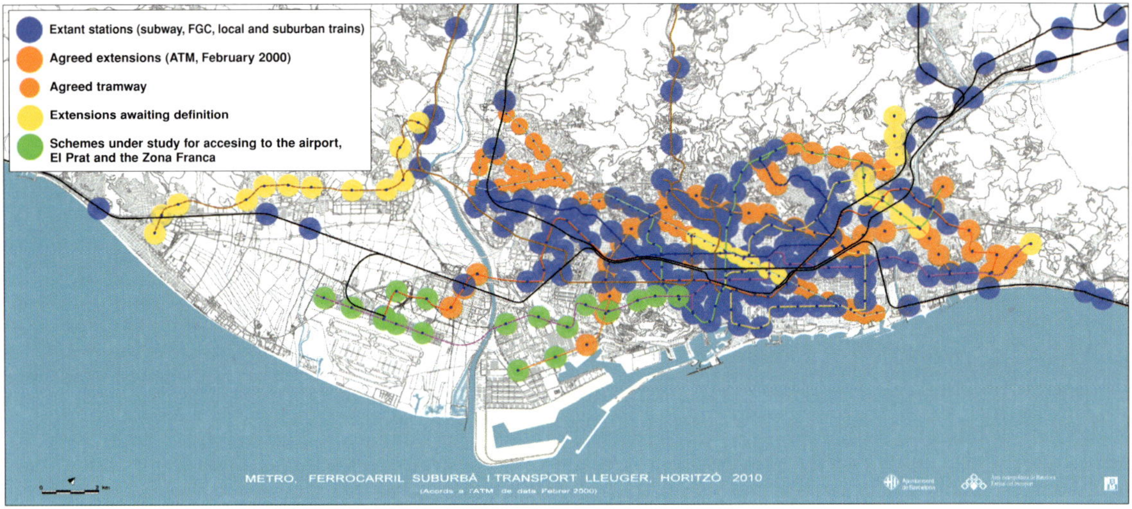

Extant stations (subway, FGC, local and suburban trains)
Agreed extensions (ATM, February 2000)
Agreed tramway
Extensions awaiting definition
Schemes under study for accesing to the airport, El Prat and the Zona Franca
METRO, FERROCARRIL SUBURBÀ I TRANSPORT LLEUGER, HORITZÓ 2010
(Acords a l'ATM de data Febrer 2000)

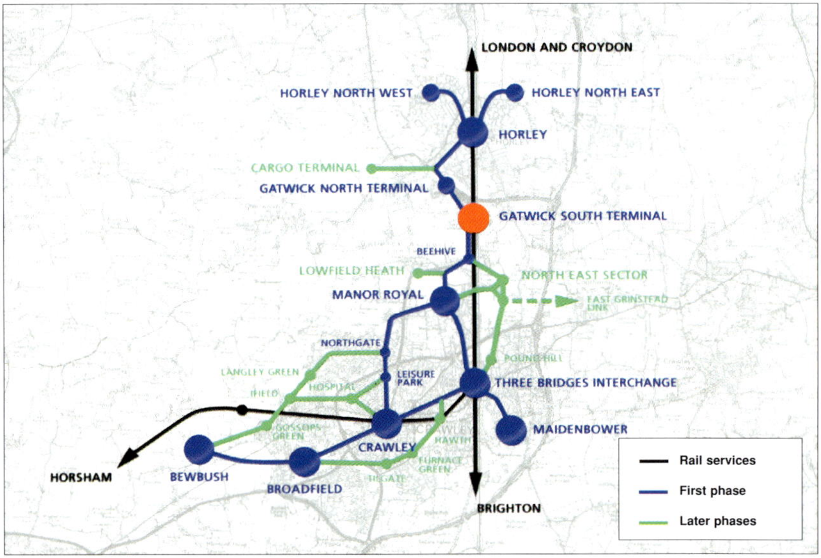

LONDON AND CROYDON
HORLEY NORTH WEST
HORLEY NORTH EAST
HORLEY
CARGO TERMINAL
GATWICK NORTH TERMINAL
GATWICK SOUTH TERMINAL
BEEHIVE
LOWFIELD HEATH
NORTH EAST SECTOR
MANOR ROYAL
EAST GRINSTEAD LINK
NORTHGATE
POUND HILL
LANGLEY GREEN
LEISURE PARK
HOSPITAL
THREE BRIDGES INTERCHANGE
IFIELD
GOSSOPS GREEN
MAIDENBOWER
CRAWLEY
FURNACE GREEN
HORSHAM
BEWBUSH
BROADFIELD
BRIGHTON
Rail services
First phase
Later phases

Barcelona's subway system will integrate the airport.
As a prerequisite for their agreement on the development of a future airport city, the Metropolitan Area of Barcelona has demanded accessibility by subway to the entire airport platform, in order to provide the same standards as in other urban developments.

Fastway: an initiative of the airport operator for a local bus network.

Airports as public transport operators

Similar initiatives are also launched by the airport operators themselves, particularly those with an entrepreneurial business outlook —operators like the BAA or the Schiphol Group, who are experienced in integral airport development concepts. They have set up their own local transport services to improve the connections to the population centres where the airport workforce lives, and to guarantee the recruitment of employees. This is an increasingly difficult task, as airport staff housing can be very far away from the airport.

The BAA's "Fastway" and the Schiphol Group's "Sternet" bus services link all airport sites to the airport station and to the population centres near to the airport, thus making the airport the focal point of a whole new local transport system with a radius of some 10 km. Arlanda Airport is studying an extension to its "SkyCab" people mover system from the terminal area to the future on-airport business park some 2 km to the south, and further on to Arlandastad and Märsta. For commuters in general, these are new attractive feeder systems into the airport station.

Pollution limits

These interventions by the airport operators are neither signs of a general goodwill nor self-motivated initiatives. Today, all major airport investments for expanding capacity have to undergo environmental impact assessment. Where the adverse environmental impacts of air traffic and airport-related road traffic are subject to a common pollution limit, the operators are urged to provide alternatives to car use to the platform employees. In Stockholm such a "maximum pollution limit" has been introduced, in view of the third runway now under construction. It has proved to be an important tool for the successful implementation of an extensive range of public transport alternatives at Arlanda Airport. Due to the government's yoking of pollution from aircraft with landside transport to and from the airport, the airport had the choice of cutting flights or reducing the landside pollution caused by car traffic. Together with Sigtuna and Arlandastad, it promotes public transport and reduces car use in the area, while pursuing more or less unconstrained growth on the airside.

A platform-focused approach versus a regional one

Being keen to exploit any possibility in order to maximise income, airport operators tend to use even the areas peripheral to their platforms. By favouring a "platform-focused" approach, many leftover areas of their restricted territory are promoted as potential business parks or sites for their own staff. Examples are the Lufthansa headquarters in Frankfurt, some 1.5 km west of the station; the Schiphol business parks 3 and 5 km north of the station, respectively; Zurich Airport's "Unique 1" building, the new administrative headquarters on the far side of the runways.

But, is the airport site really that attractive? It seems that a lot of these projects benefit from the fact that the territory is under less land use control than elsewhere. This outweighs the handicap of their not necessarily being prime sites. In many cases, these sites are as yet only accessible by car or airport shuttle bus, and are also less accessible than potential development sites within the airport surroundings.

The question arises as to whether strategies for common site development outside the airport territory, together with newly established regional rail services, should not be considered more often as an alternative. Regional public transport initiatives around airports form the basis for a more "regional" approach to airport development. An airport city is not limited to the airport. Airport city planning does not stop at the airport perimeter. This would, however, require co-operation between the airport operator and the municipality across the boundaries of their respective territories. The problem is that to think —let alone to operate— on the other side of the airport perimeter —in whichever direction— is still terra incognita. Both airport operators and local authorities are unfamiliar with how to work together in the creation of an airport city. Unresolved questions such as how airport operators can raise real estate income outside their own territory are still major obstacles.

Due to the controversial reactions of local authorities to recent business plans by the airport operators on their own platforms in Schiphol, Frankfurt and Zurich, agreements regarding co-ordinated off-airport development seem to be just a matter of time.

Zurich's new "Stadtbahn" light-rail system will accentuate a ribbon of high-value urban development in the Glattal, all of this within easy reach of the airport.

Line of light-rail with stops (according to the regional plan of the canton)

Additional stops

Hinterland of light-rail stops (radius of 300m)

Existing

Development areas

Green areas

6. Airport hardware

Aerial view

Paris Roissy-Charles de Gaulle Airport

The core sectors of the airport business are airline handling, passenger transport, freight transport and related commercial activities. Air traffic growth means that landing and parking aircraft, and moving people around, becomes increasingly complex. The design of the airside becomes an increasingly sophisticated undertaking. In order to make way for new, less technocratically conceived concepts, it is important to understand the mechanics of what is proper airport design, the layout of the airside.

Runway capacity

To accommodate ever more air traffic, airports need to be able to operate several runways simultaneously. As aircraft are becoming less sensitive to crosswind, runways are nowadays preferably set up in parallel, which allows for the greatest number of slots (landings and takeoffs). Due to turbulence behind incoming and outgoing aircraft, the minimum distance between runways should be no less than 1,350m. The preferred location for terminals is between the runways, allowing planes to easily access fingers or aprons without having to taxi across the parallel runway.

Terminal capacity

Terminal capacity is firstly determined by the length of the line of transition between airside and landside, and secondly by the number of gates available at piers. The continual need for more terminal capacity leads to spider-shaped, telescopic terminals (AMS, VIE), to the creation of multi-terminal systems (LGW, LHR, FRA, ARN, BCN), or to the creation of satellites connected to the main terminal by a people mover (often underground) (CDG, ZRH, MXP).

The sheer size (or length) of the terminals of an airport of 20 million passengers per annum or more makes it difficult to operate from one central core. The distances to be covered are becoming too long (2km in Amsterdam between gates H and B), and hence other internal accessibility concepts are required. Two basic concepts have emerged: an internal people mover, as at LGW and FRA; or more than one railway station, as at ARN with three, or LHR with five. This concept appears especially valid for trains that explicitly serve the airport (the Arlanda Express, Malpensa Express, Heathrow Express).

Dedicated terminals

In the United States, main airlines have built their own terminals (e.g. JFK). Most European airports, on the other hand, feature terminals serving all airline companies simultaneously, as air traffic liberalisation nowadays encourages free access to terminals for all companies. However, airlines and particularly airline alliances are beginning to demand dedicated terminals (long lease), in order to reduce connection times for transfer passengers (part of the hub concept) and to improve passenger convenience. At Frankfurt Airport, the new Terminal A has been developed exclusively for the Star Alliance, and was financed jointly by Lufthansa and the airport. With the anticipated consolidation between the thirteen national carriers in the European airline industry, dedicated terminals are becoming part of the power game for control over airport design. Airlines will increasingly demand them in exchange for using an airport as an operational base.

In principle, the continual growth and reorganisation of terminal facilities should not make dedicated terminals difficult to attain. Split terminals, however, make landside access to all terminals inef-

One-terminal (telescope)

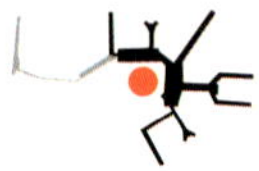

AMS

Multi-terminal

FRA

Satellite

ZRH

Modular

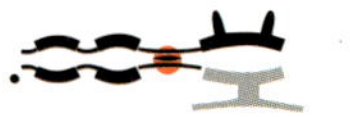

CDG

Different terminal concepts, all of them based on flexibility for expansion.

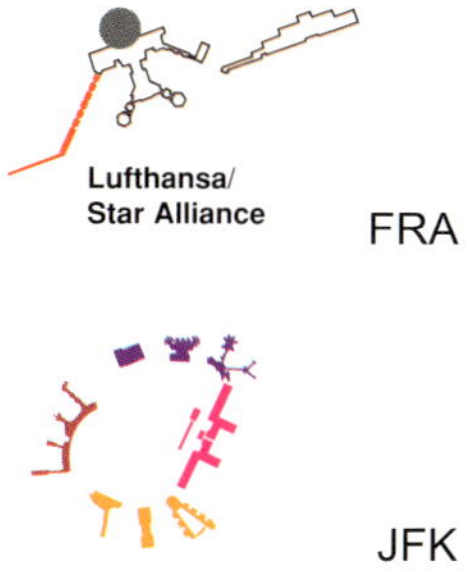

Airline alliances demand dedicated terminals. JFK and FRA (with the new Star Alliance terminal) respond to it.

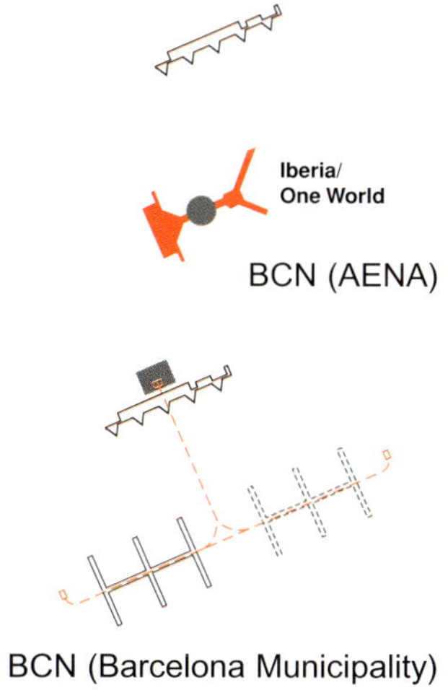

The terminal designs for BCN Airport reflect the potentially different positions of an airport and a city: AENA aims at maximising the efficiency for Iberia and its One World partner as the main customers, with a dedicated new terminal. BR's design opts for flexibility in the long term with a satellite giving equal rights to all airline companies.

ficient and often extremely complex. Among other things, this jeopardises the ambition to reduce transfer times between air traffic and High Speed Trains, and thus to make the most of AiRail synergy.

A new generation of terminal buildings

The centre of an airport used to be the departure hall located between the parking lots and the apron area. Increased air traffic led to expansion of the departure hall, and eventually to the realisation of several halls, sometimes in the form of split terminals.

Increased integration in public transport networks, with its concomitant landside interchange development, plus the growing percentage of transfer passengers on the airside, introduces a new trend in terminal organisation, visible in both the transformation of existing terminals and the design of completely new ones. Given the size of these terminals, and thus the long distances to be covered, terminal functions are decentralised. The central departure and arrival hall, where all transfer and check-in activities once took place, is gradually replaced by a concept of two well-connected poles in the terminal area:

• The railway station: a multi-modal interchange

The railway station, or multi-modal interchange, is a regional interface. When railways began serving airports, the station was usually set as close as possible to the departure hall (short and fast lanes for passengers). In certain cases, however, the arrival of the railway had a much stronger impact: it led to a reorganisation of the terminal, making the station hall the centre of the airport (AMS). This trend is repeated in many airports today. The station hall —or interchange— becomes one of the core elements for airside passenger operations as well, since it includes terminal functions like check-in facilities and baggage claim for air passenger convenience. The interest of airport operators in a convenient and beautiful station grows.

Schiphol rail station (triangular red roof) in the terminals core.

• The airside centre

The airside centre, where a distribution of passengers between the satellites, peripheral fingers, etc., takes place, is an internal interface for transfer passengers.

The growth of the airside into a big and often complex system, with various terminals or satellites, and the occasional need of shuttles or people movers to connect them, has led to the desire for a switchboard, a central unit co-ordinating passenger movement through the airport, this unit itself being a common lounge. Airside centres were and are introduced in a position that allows for quick and efficient connection to all passenger areas, and particularly to the interchange, the other pole. Transit between the two becomes crucial: ZRH and FRA feature direct pedestrian connections.

The new Airside Centre at Zurich Airport (the vaulted roof between the two piers).

Both poles concentrate flows of people, and are therefore attractive to commercial and business enterprises. Both are being cashed in on by the operator. The airside centre evolves as the airport's core for shopping, eating, leisure and lounge facilities. The railway station acquires an importance for the airport's landside similar to that of any major interchange node in the metropolitan area (e.g. the central station) vis-à-vis its urban surroundings. It is a trigger for development.

7. The downtown airport

Aerial view

Vienna Airport

It is in the very nature of airports for them to be out-of-date before their most recent renovation is over. Forever catching up with the overcoming of capacity constraints, the next construction phase seamlessly complements the one before. The most successful terminal layouts are therefore those which allow for continual expansion. An enforced halt to building is every airport's nightmare, and —measured against the growth predictions for air traffic— is perceived as being synonymous with a radical fall in international ranking: an imminent end to the chances of being a "relevant European air traffic platform" is involved here.

Inherent to the new business strategies of airport operators is that both their real estate activities and the injection of additional commercial programmes within the terminals has to occur at the same speed as investment in the expansion of airside facilities. Otherwise, their margin of profit would further decrease, taking on board the need to keep landing fees and airport taxes low in order to remain competitive. This correlation makes air traffic growth extremely physical: there is a direct "urban" output, a continual increase in commercial and business floor space built on the landside of the terminals.

To avoid saturation of the latter, the same flexibility as provided for airside expansion begins to dominate strategies for landside development. Driven by technological and social changes on the airside, and a new business reality on the landside, airports find ways to expand further, not only at the far end of the mile-long piers, but also on the landside of the platform's centre.

Airports advertise themselves as highly dynamic places. The airport's inherent restlessness, and the fact that things change faster here, qualifies this location in relation to other areas of the city. The Amsterdam Airport slogan "Schiphol is building for the future" is iconic in this respect. Present in all the airport piers under construction, it is a euphoric sign of future perfection. Ironically, this change factor —and thus the only prospect for optimal operation— has been adopted as a slogan for up-to-date airport operation and customer service quality...

KLM blamed Schiphol Airport for "obstructing the way for our passengers with their shopping public. If you want to reach our lounge, you get there only via a sharing stand." Irritation about the fact "that Schiphol decides what happens on Schiphol" has recently culminated in KLM's threat to sue the airport for some 30M Euros for the damage suffered due to insufficient and inconvenient service.

Airside centre or airside shopping centre

The new commercially oriented approach to airport operation has radically altered terminal design.

Terminal buildings are seen in retailing terms: money dictates the layout. This condition leads to a power game between main airline and airport, the main carrier's home base. While the ongoing commercialisation of airports proves to be a goldmine for the airport operator, it causes more and more headaches for the home carrier. To the operator, the absurdity of passenger trajectories through the terminals —a reminder of continuous adaptation to their performance— now seems a commercial advantage. Distances are no longer a burden; instead they have become profitable. In that respect airport development does not differ much from that of the central station, where traveller convenience is challenged by shops aggressively invading the circulation space with furniture, garish lights and obtrusive smells. Stations like Zurich CS and Liverpool Street, however, offer an alternative by giving circulation and commercial activities their own separate levels.

Schiphol is currently busy with the second phase of its own airport city: a massive densification (orange) of the urban strip.

Terminal city

The overall layout of Amsterdam Airport makes the different generations of airport design clearly legible. This began in the 1960s with a terminal concept that proved to be almost endlessly expandable until today. Next, with the construction of a main central plaza on

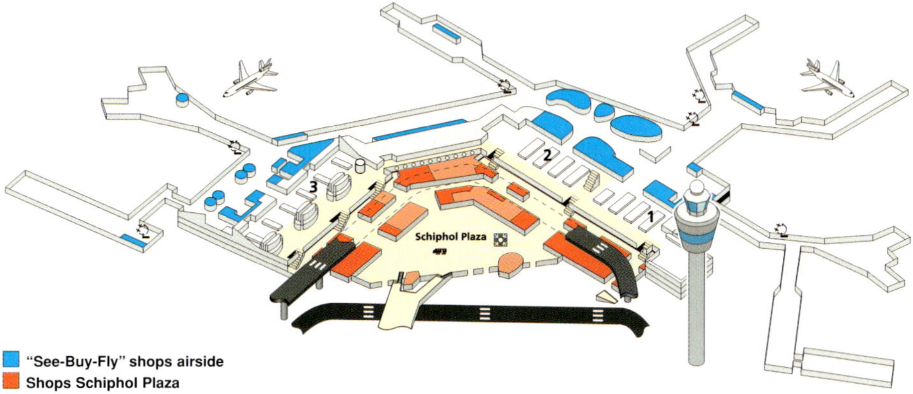
3
2
1
Schiphol Plaza
"See-Buy-Fly" shops airside
Shops Schiphol Plaza

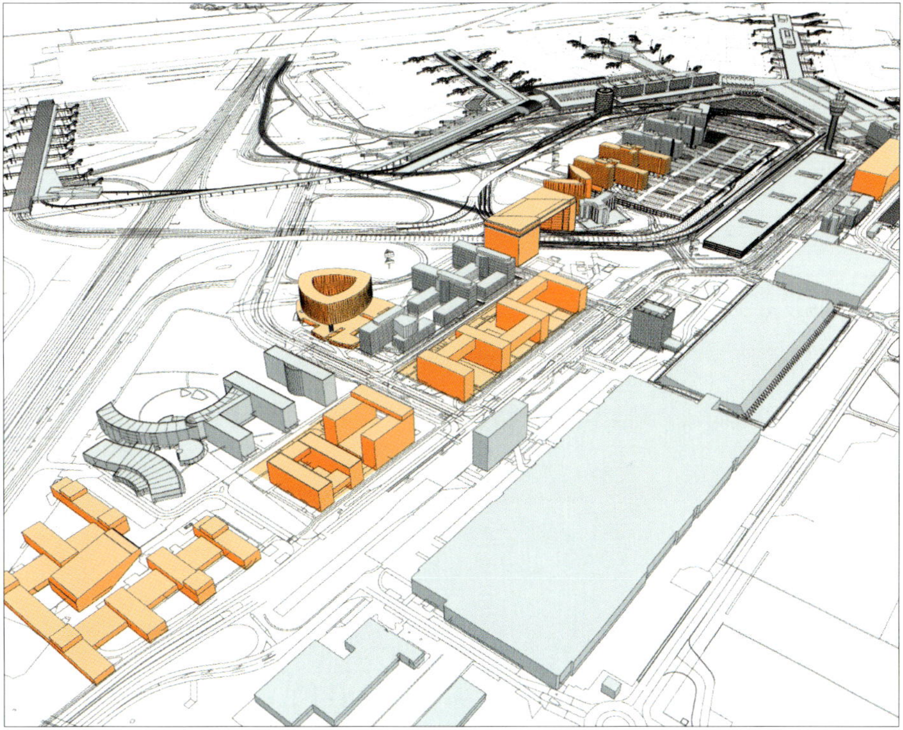

top of the railway station in the early 1990s, a re-concentration in the centre of the terminal constellation occurred. The third generation of airport design embraces an urban masterplan for the landside, a 2km-long strip stretching from the station to the highway exit, to allow for accommodating the urban programme and output near to the station.

Winning entry (Baumschlager & Eberle, Itten + Brechbühl) for an urban planning competition for VIE's airport city.

The design strategy of this strip seems to mirror the laws of terminal design on the landside. The same sprawl as is visible on the airside also determines the landside. In the form of numerous additions, as in air terminal construction, the airport city is conceived along a backbone of *tapis roulants*: a WTC for global front offices, a Sheraton Hotel, a Hilton, the headquarters of the Schiphol Group, of SADC, an aviodome, etc. The plan is realised step by step, building by building, upon demand or when additional income is required. Schiphol has created its own golden rule in this respect: for each additional million passengers, 10,000 m² of office space are to be built on its territory. The upshot of this pragmatic approach is an additive, but highly adaptable, plan.

A piece of city

In the competition for its new masterplan, Vienna Airport recently gave its top award to a scheme that attempts to overcome the logic of infrastructural planning at airports. This scheme proposes a fictitious airside/landside harmony for the central area of the platform. The masterplan tries to combine the requirements of terminal expansion with a desire to establish a "city look" on its landside. Offices, garages and hotels are arranged to form an "urban environment" which will soon consist of streets and squares. Is this an image more appropriate to the economic reality of airport operation?

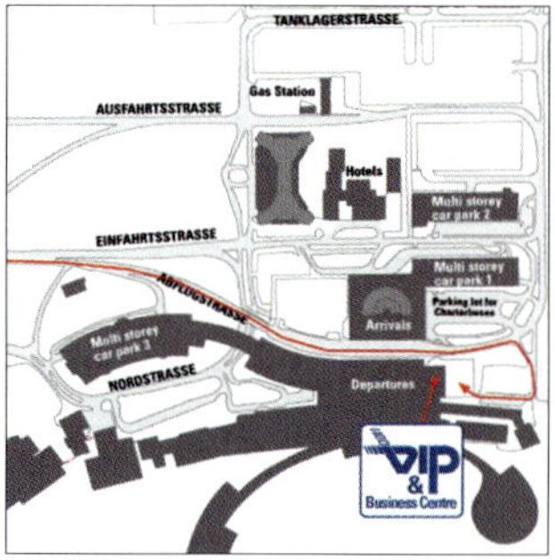

The forecourt of the terminals of Vienna Airport today: a jumble of roads and parking.

A discreet airport city

The platform on top of Frankfurt Airport's ICE-station is ready for an enormous super-block of commercial activities, as a railway-station development.

Unlike Schiphol or, more recently, Vienna Airport, which advertise and promote the airport city concept, Fraport, the operator of Frankfurt Airport, has been much more cautious during the last fifteen years. The situation there requires strict co-operation between the airport and the local authorities. The fact that the airport lies just within the boundaries of the city — and within the "sacred" city forest— has meant that Frankfurt has insisted on the airport being just an airport; that is, an airport to serve the region. The city's resistance to any major commercial real estate development on the airport platform is very strong. Given these constraints, Fraport has had to come up with innovative and highly concentrated forms of landside development.

The first generation of its discreet airport city is a compact hotel and conference centre, erected on top of the regional railway station and squeezed in among enormous parking buildings. The dimensions of the Sheraton, with its 1,050 rooms, plus their equivalent in conference capacity, are unique in Europe. They are more than twice the size of the chain's establishments at Charles de Gaulle or Schiphol Airports.

The second generation of Frankfurt's airport city is even more interesting. Fraport is building a 170,000 m² business and commercial centre, using only the site on top of the new HST station. For the realisation of the 8-9-storey complex, containing two hotels, a medical care centre, an office area, major commercial surfaces and 1,000 parking spaces, major pre-investment in the form of a 660m-long deck above the tracks was necessary. With these dimensions, Fraport's AIRail terminal is bigger than the real estate developments so proudly advertised as airport cities by its major competitors. Schiphol has created some 150,000 m² of offices in its centre and

Winning entry (developer: AIRRAIL Center Frankfurt GmbH, design: J.S.K. International) of the AIRail terminal competition.

Vienna opts for 50,000 m² of office space in its overall plan.

Rather than appearing as an airport city, however, the new AIRail terminal at Frankfurt Airport is a central station development. Given the sensibilities of the Frankfurt authorities, this compact structure is limited to the space above the tracks and does not compete with the skyscrapers dominating the inner city skyline. Since WW2 bombing wiped out the centre of Frankfurt, emotions are still running high about rebuilding the area around the Central Station as the new emblem of the city's regained self-confidence. For all that, the AIRail terminal found its way into an advertisement for the airport. There it is presented as the truly outstanding building project of Frankfurt's financial centre.

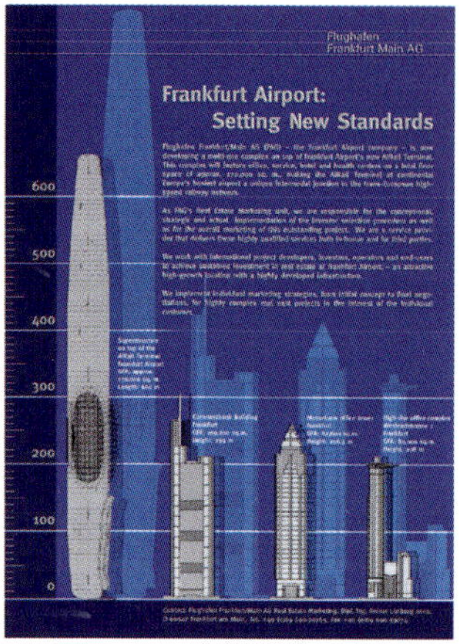

Frankfurt Airport advertises its 660m-long AIRail terminal by comparing it with the tallest and newest skyscrapers of downtown Frankfurt.

Hybrid Airports

The new generation of airport masterplans almost always have strategies for real estate development, to the rear of and opposite the terminals. But the creation of an airport city at the core of the airport cannot be subordinated to the same infrastructural logic as the terminals. The logic of building a city at the airport's railway station is different. Is it possible to propose a new typology for such terminals? Can an answer be found to the increasingly ambivalent condition of airports? Can we break with the duality of airport design: office parks on the one side, and telescopic terminal megastructures equipped with kilometers-long travelators on the other? The hybrid airport fully integrates the twin realities of airport operation: flying and doing business. It is not about designing a city around a terminal. It proposes designing a terminal around a limited, hyper-efficient city — without constraining the elasticity that is decisive for the long-term operability of airports.

The authors' team's competition entry for the expansion of Frankfurt Airport on its former US airbase: a compact terminal setup for 25M passengers with a limited airport city integrated in, and not added to, it. The interchange node to the north will remain the epicentre of the airport.

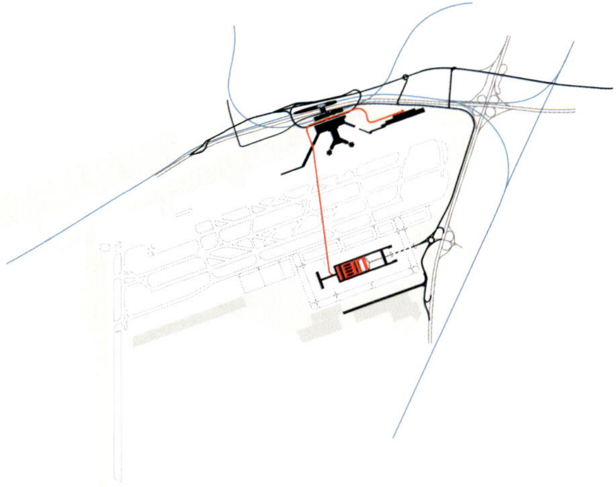

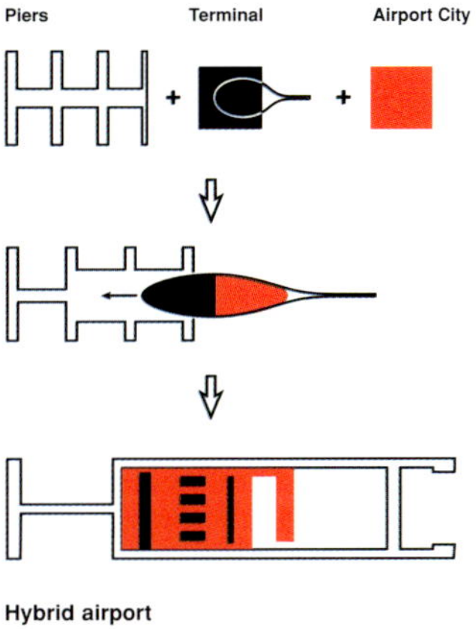
Piers
Terminal
Airport City
Hybrid airport

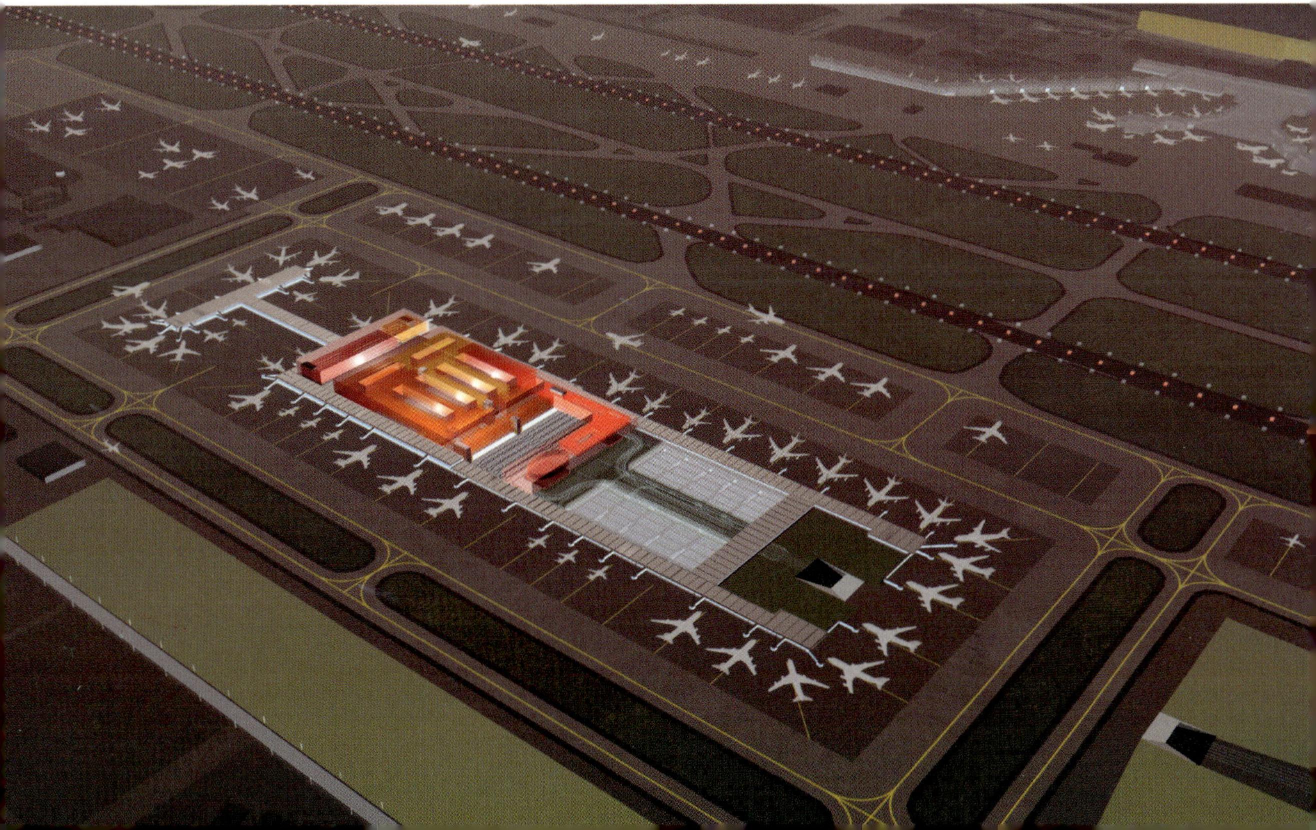

The hybrid airport breaks with the additive nature of airport layouts. It addresses modularity without an endlessly repeatable high-tech roof; its flexibility is inherent to its urban plan. It incorporates, rather than accommodates, the programme attracted by the airport's particular infrastructural condition.

The hybrid airport is no final or definitive typology, but a reflection of the cultural change in the operation and use of the airport.

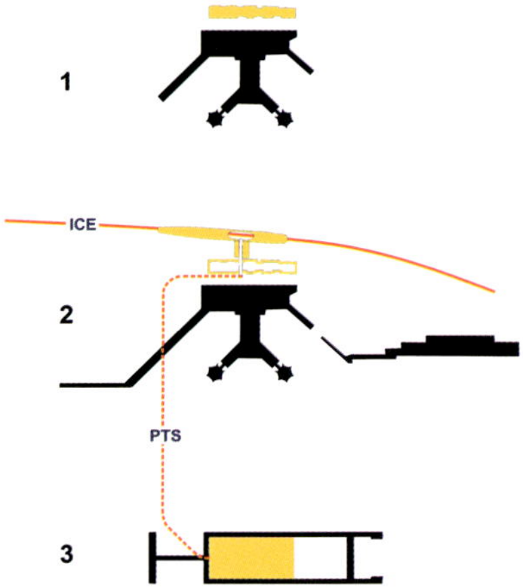

1. The first generation of real estate development on top of the regional rail station: Sheraton and conference centre.

2. The second-generation AIRail terminal sits on top of the HST station.

3. The third generation could be inside a new satellite terminal: Fraport administration, hotel, conference and entertainment facilities.

To once again propose a particularly transport-efficient airport city for Frankfurt meant that it would have to sit on top of the main people mover station of the new terminal.

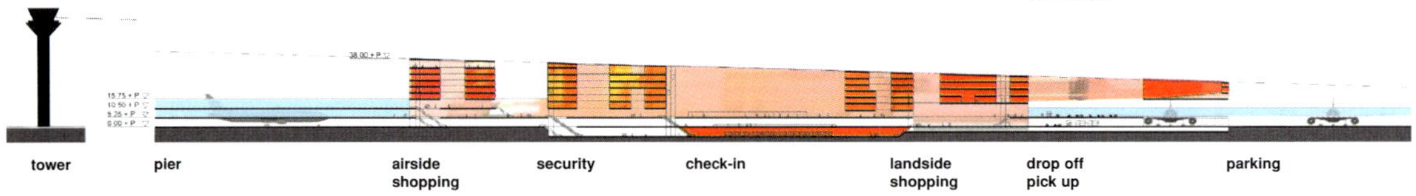

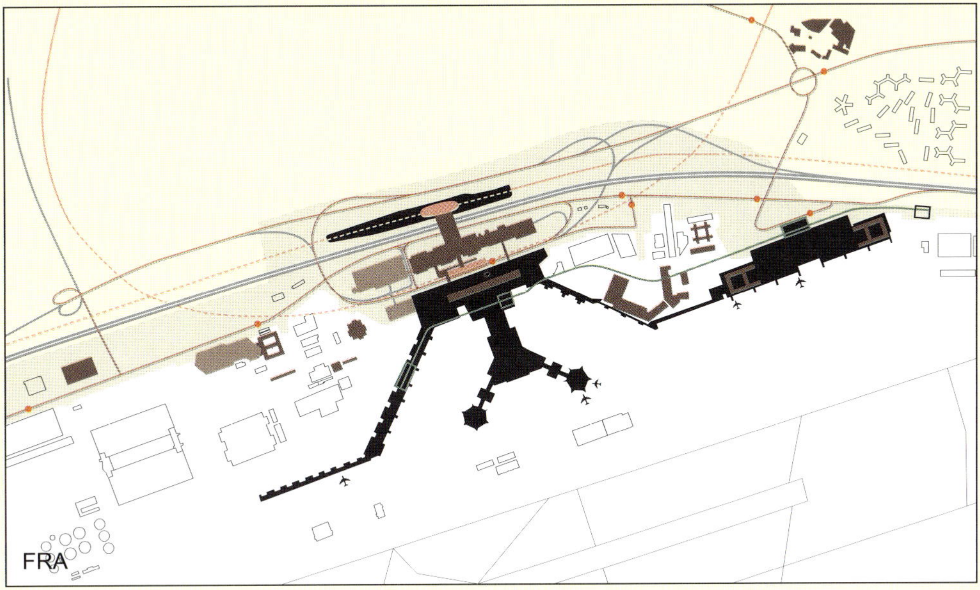
FRA

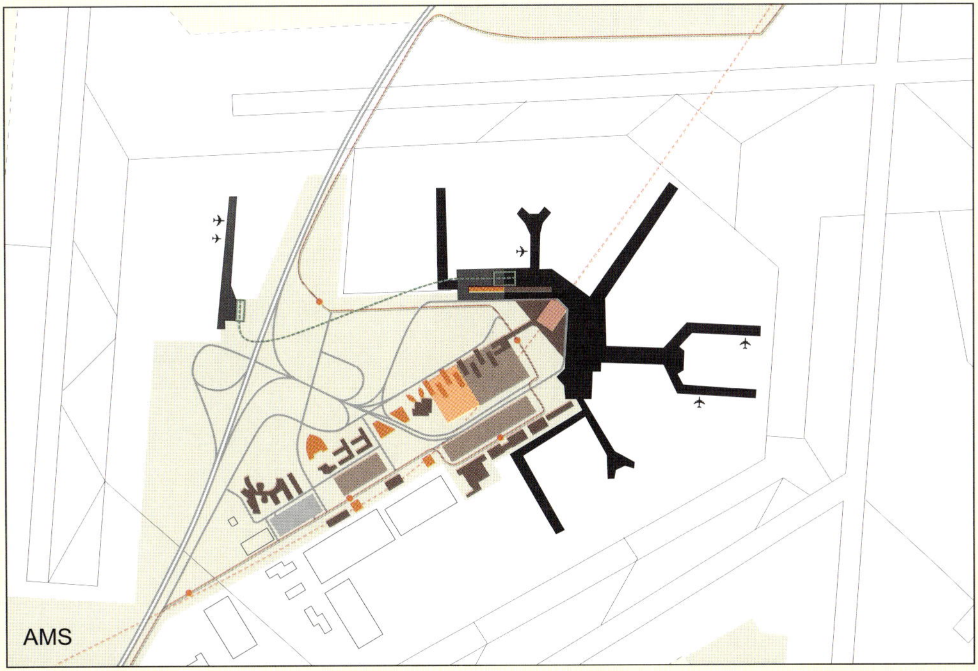
AMS

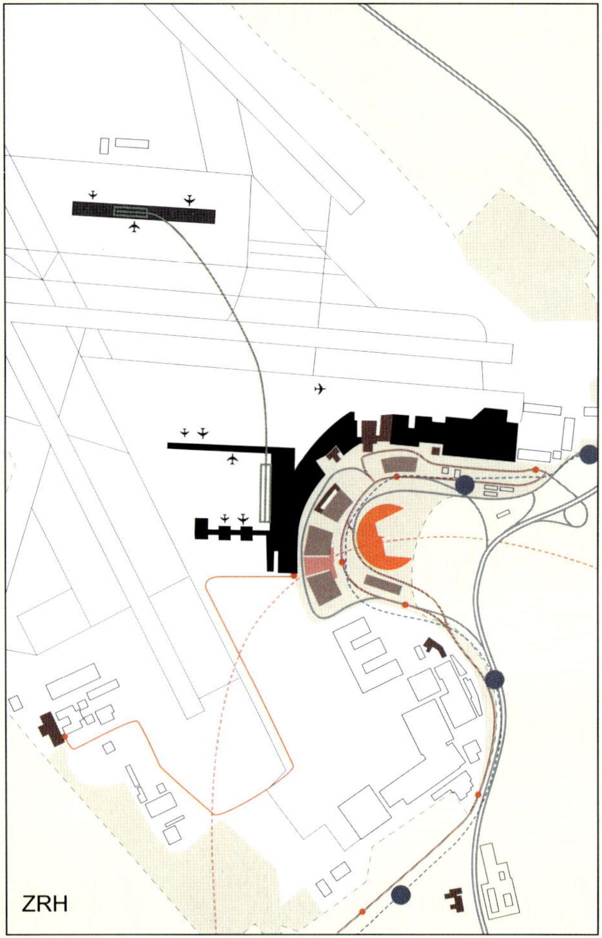
ZRH

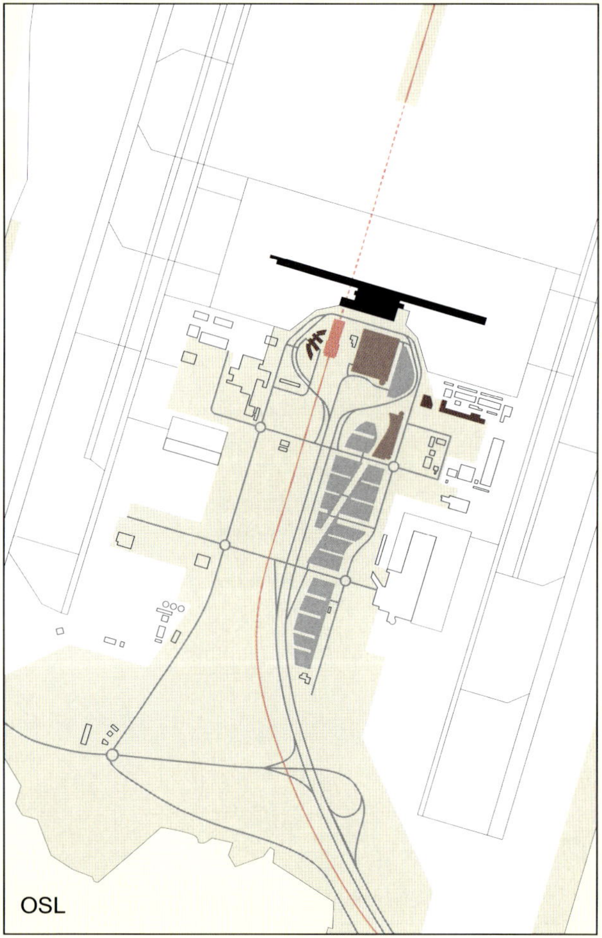
OSL

The ideas of airports for building their own bit of airport city vary radically.

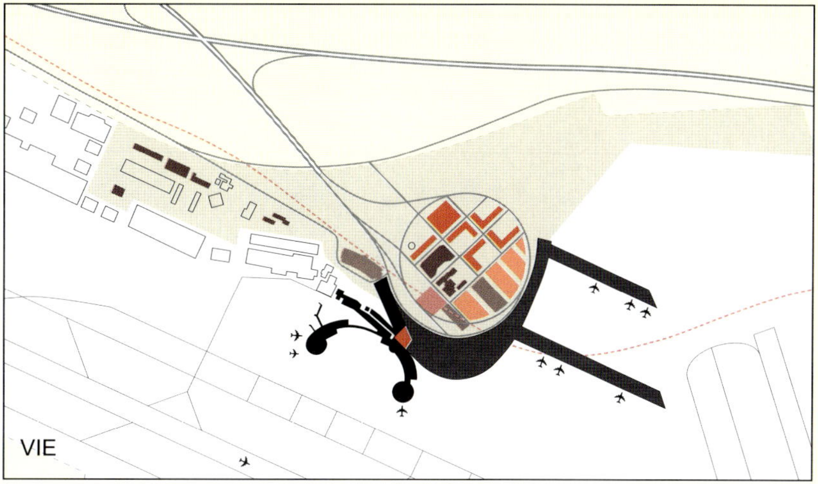

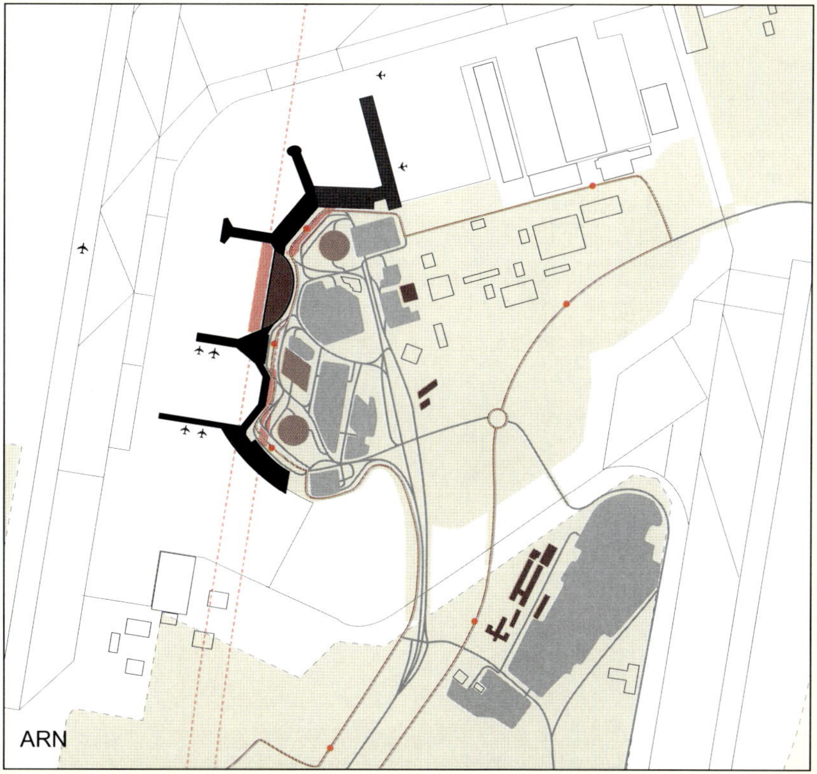

8. The domain of the airport

Aerial view

Barcelona Airport

Airports are often perceived as entities with their own rules, their own dynamic, their own legitimacy; entities that are beyond the control of local and regional authorities. On closer inspection, however, airports are not so segregated from what goes on around them any more. The parameters have changed.

Analysis of the contemporary condition of the airport reveals an urgent need to rethink airport design. If the airport evolves into an airport city, it should be planned as if it were a city, not just a runway, a terminal and a parking lot. If multi-modal connections to the hinterland are created, the terminal should be reconceived as a regional interchange, not just a departure hall. These two in-airport trends offer points of contact to hook up with, points where local and regional involvement becomes interesting and possible. Today, airports are far from being closed entities.

Airport cities are fashionable —from Barcelona to Helsinki, from Vienna to Amsterdam. They are being put up extremely quickly, all but proportionally to the increase in aviation movement, and driven by the opportunities for cashing in on real estate development around airports, as compensation for the enormous investment in airport infrastructure. In spite of this evident trend, one is not yet sure how to design or conceive airport cities. Airports are still laid out by engineers. Most plans for these "cities" are still drawn up by a transport operator, the airport. If no other measures are taken, this is likely to happen without the participation of the regional and local authorities. Nobody foresaw the success of airports in establishing a new identity, and planning authorities have been unable to invent and implement strategies at the speed required by air traffic evolution.

Airport design was once a purely aeronautical matter. But as the airport concept is adjusted and stretched beyond measure — in terms of image, rules and development— the landside aspect becomes ever more crucial and has a major influence on the choices made. As airport operators pursue this new airport typology, the most disconcerting question in regional terms becomes: is the kind of "city" growing at the airport desirable for the metropolitan region as a whole? The various proposals for Barcelona Airport, or the current discussions about variations to terminal models for Helsinki Airport, reveal that airport planning can no longer be considered as a blank sheet — as "none of my business". Joint strategies for landside development have to be sought by the airport and the metropolitan area together.

"Historically", airports were run and developed by state authorities. National air traffic policies endowed airports with a special status on their territory, giving them a certain operational freedom. Today, airports redefine their domain themselves. The primary task remains that of guaranteeing the efficiency of the core business: the facilitating of air traffic. Today, however, airports claim that their current domain not only consists of runways, but includes major real estate development.

As airports forego the role of simple operator and opt for building airport cities, the limits to the airport's domain are being challenged: does their special status also apply to airport city development? Who is responsible for designing and governing this "city"? If an airport works as a city, does it require new organisational structures and new forms of collaboration, corporate structures rather than market forces?

Local and regional authorities do not have much influence on the way airports are run, nor on air traffic growth in the long term. On the other hand, they do have experience in spatial planning, thus

1

1930

2

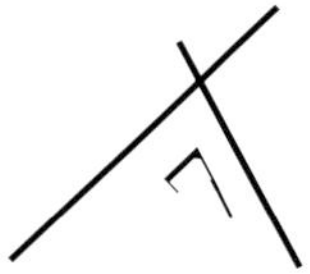

HEL 1960

As airports leave the realm of an airfield behind, tasks change:

1 to build an airfield

2 to build runways in all possible wind directions

3

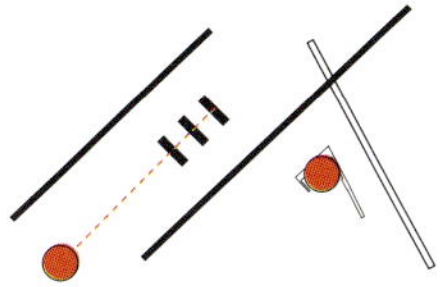

HEL future

4

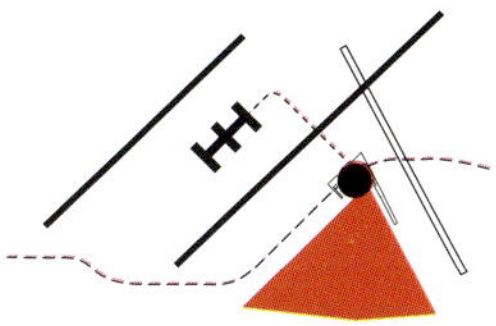

HEL future

3 to tune the terminal concept with the appropriate position of the rail station
4 to build an airport city and integrate it with the airport interchange
Does the domain change accordingly?

enabling them to set standards for the efficient integration of airport cities and interchange nodes. But, in order to be able to participate in the creation of a contemporary airport, and in particular of an airport city development, it is urgent for local and regional authorities to understand the mechanisms and rules of airside development as well as airport organisation. These are the parameters that airport operators consider as they develop an overall masterplan that includes both the airside and landside in equal measure. As airports begin getting involved beyond their own territory, so public authorities will have to think about what happens within the latter. The airport perimeter ceases to be a boundary within which decisions are to be taken by the airport operator alone. When it comes to the renovation and expansion of airside facilities, the surrounding authorities need to get involved. At the same time, the involvement of the airport operator beyond its own territory will become ever more common. Not all the features of a 21st-century airport (city) will find a place within the limits of the "technical area", and real estate development within the airport surroundings is a very attractive source of additional income for the airport operator too.

Any insistence on the original airport concept —a planning enclave behind a fence— would inevitably lead to major tension between operators and authorities, particularly in cases where these questions are not carefully dealt with prior to the process of privatisation.

AENA and Barcelona: operator and city

Following the modernisation of Barcelona Airport for the 1992 Olympic Games, AENA, Spain's Civil Airport Administration, and Iberia, the state-owned airline, shifted their attention to further

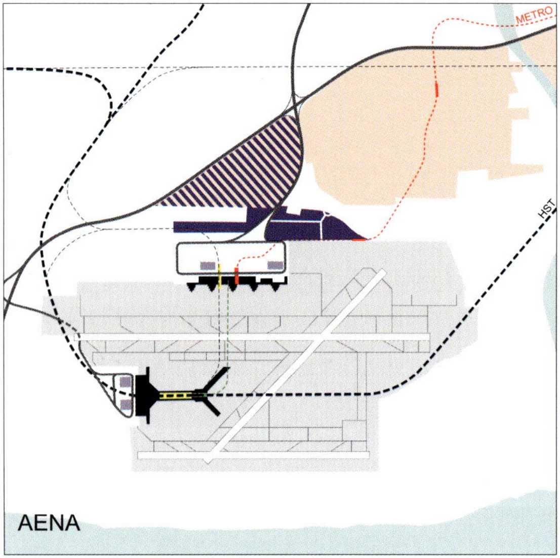

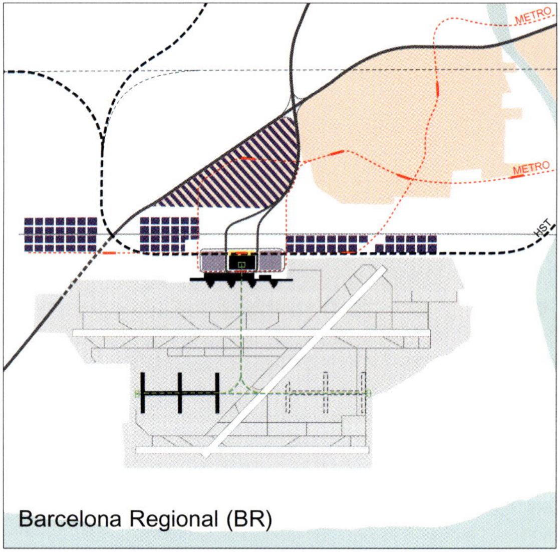

AENA's new terminal design provides maximum passenger convenience for the majority of passengers, but needs two highway accesses and two major parking areas. It makes do with the fact that the airport city and its employees and visitors are completely remote from the main terminal and thus have no convenient direct access to the new rail station.

The airport city concept of the City of Barcelona integrates terminal, rail station interchange, operational facilities, airport-related activities and new landside developments, all in one area. A series of subway stops guarantees high accessibility to all zones. This concept makes do with the fact that the majority of origin and destination passengers will have to use a people mover between the existing terminal and the new midfield satellites.

Barcelona's main terminal today: the main terminal also in BR's proposal for 25-30M passengers, with midfield satellites accommodating the growth beyond. In AENA's proposal this terminal is first expanded in order to handle up to 25M passengers, but will be resized to 10-15M as soon as the new main terminal between runways is operative. The latter will have a capacity to handle 30-40M passengers a year.

developing Madrid Barajas Airport. Therefore, both the Autonomous Government of Catalonia and Barcelona City Hall (through its metropolitan planning agency Barcelona Regional BR) launched their own initiatives regarding the future of the airport. When in 1999 AENA resumed the development of strategies for Barcelona Airport, it found itself in an unusual, if not unique, situation in European terms: it found itself up against two public authorities with very clear (but somewhat different) ideas as to the development of their airport and its role in the region.

BCN Airport is expected to reach its capacity limit by 2005. Operational facilities are underdeveloped; ancillary activities are as yet non-existent. Accessibility via public transport is poor, not least because taxi services account for 45% of passenger trips to and from the airport. The next expansion plan will first have to solve the problem of aviation bottlenecks. An additional parallel runway is to be built. Terminal capacity will be more than doubled —between the runways. Operational and cargo facilities will be brought up to standard. The expansion plan also includes building a major railway station and creating an airport city, both from scratch: at present there is neither an interchange nor an airport city.

Opinions about how this should be done differed. AENA aimed to optimise the airport as a technical and operational facility. BR's main goal was to integrate both the airport and the impact of its expansion within the metropolitan area.

A satellite or multi-terminal scheme

BR considered that opportunities for airport-related landside development depended largely on the new terminal concept. It proposed to consolidate the main terminal in its present location and to directly integrate it with the airport city, and to build satellite docks in the midfield area. This terminal system would be very flexible in relation to airport growth (more satellites) and to changing airline alliances.

AENA's main interest was in providing a convenient dedicated terminal for Iberia and its airline alliance, One World, both of which account for some 60-70% of BCN's current air traffic. This was considered possible only with a new terminal between runways, dedicated to One World, leaving the current terminal for the other companies.

A regional interchange or airport station

A direct HST link at the airport would enlarge its catchment area to a Euro-region of 15 million inhabitants. This was the Catalan and Barcelona governments' trump card for having the HST line diverted into and through the city, instead of having it bypass Barcelona to the north, as originally planned by the Spanish government.

The local and regional authorities intended to make the airport HST station the catalyst for a regional interchange, thus improving service not only for passengers, but also for airport employees. As a result, BR planned to locate this interchange just to the north of the existing air terminal, thereby anchoring it in the airport city and increasing the latter's attractiveness as a regional business location.

Being anxious to maximise air passenger convenience, AENA intended to locate the HST station under the main terminal between the runways. Eventually, this HST station could also be converted into a regional interchange. It would be of little use, however, for the airport city north of the existing terminal.

The airport city: annexe or state-of-the-art concept?

The airport expansion is to take BCN from today's 500 to a future 1,000 employees per million passengers. With the expected doubling of passenger figures, employee numbers will shoot up from 8,000 to 30-40,000 persons. For their activities, some 800,000 m^2 of industrial floor space —or an area of about 200 ha— are expected to be required, in addition to the 150 ha for operational facilities and logistics: truly an airport city. There is no other option than to locate this massive project to the north of the existing terminal.

BR viewed and conceived this airport city as a new piece of city within the metropolitan area, including the entire range of functions found at airports: terminals, operational facilities, airport-related businesses, hotels, conference venues, and public transport. This was not all: new standards were demanded for this generation of airport cities. The mayor of Barcelona whished to give the compact but vast area a public transport service quality matching that of any other district in his city. As a consequence, two of the city's most important subway lines were to be elongated, furnishing the airport city with up to seven conveniently located stops.

AENA conceived the northern zone as a spatial reserve for operational and logistical activities; for that reason a link to the new railway station under the midfield terminal was considered unnecessary. The scarce land to the rear of the midfield terminal could eventually be used for hotels, conference facilities and shops. This, however, would result in extra pressure on the wetland habitats and agriculture in that area.

What the confrontation yielded

The local and regional authorities' strategy for actively designing the airport expansion according to their own interests resulted in various adaptations and new considerations in the AENA expansion plan. The importance of creating an airport city with a diverse range of activities was recognised, and consensus was reached about providing urban access to both the airport and airport city by means of a series of subway stops on a new metro line to be built by the Catalan Autonomous Government. The existing commuter train line will be upgraded, with two new stations under the current as well as the new terminal. Finally, the State has agreed in 2000 to build the new HST line in a position just north of the airport, with the Catalan Government to arrange for its extension to the new terminal.

Recent political decisions, however, show how difficult it is to realize these elements. The prestigious HST station will most likely not be built at the airport, but in the airport municipality, El Prat, connected to the airport only by commuter train and metro. As of now, the regional initiative of the subway extension has been more persistent, although the line feeding the airport city has also been postponed.

To design and develop the airport masterplan, AENA has set up a special office in Barcelona without, however, including regular political and technical participation from the local and regional authorities. Participation has remained limited to consulting of the airport municipality about the preliminary urban plan.

Infrastucture

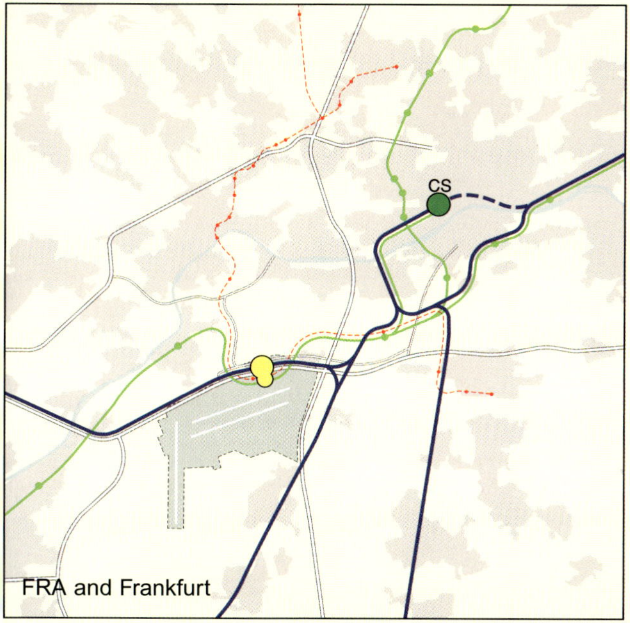

FRA and Frankfurt

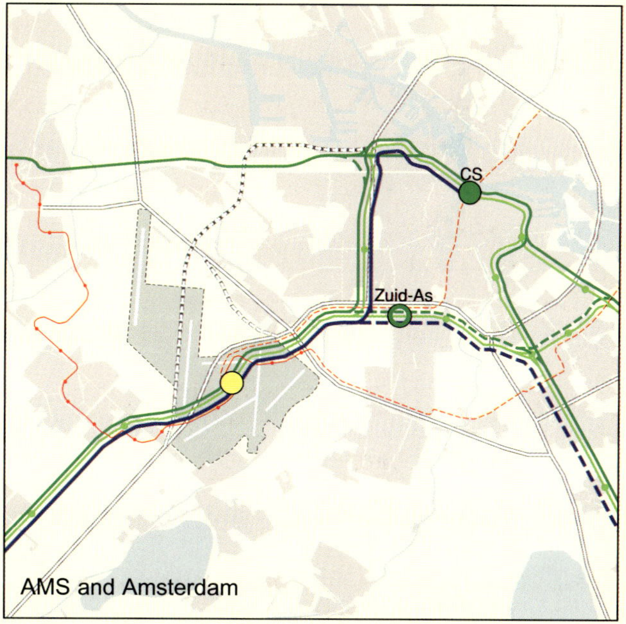

AMS and Amsterdam

LGW and Crawley

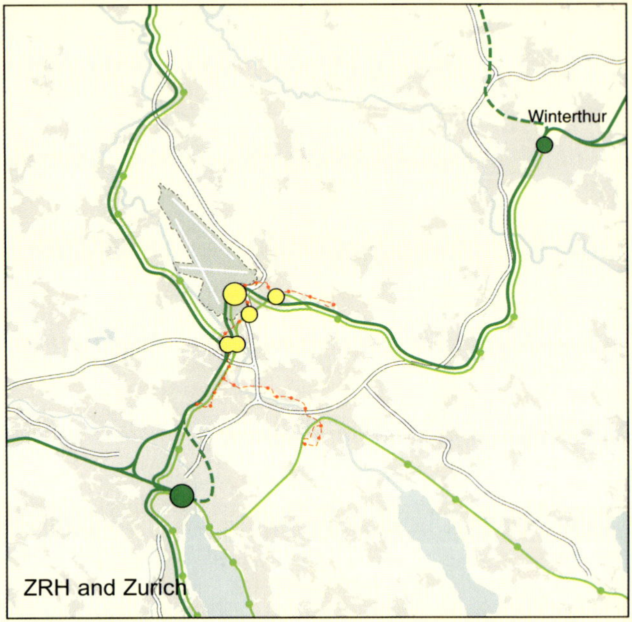
Winterthur
ZRH and Zurich

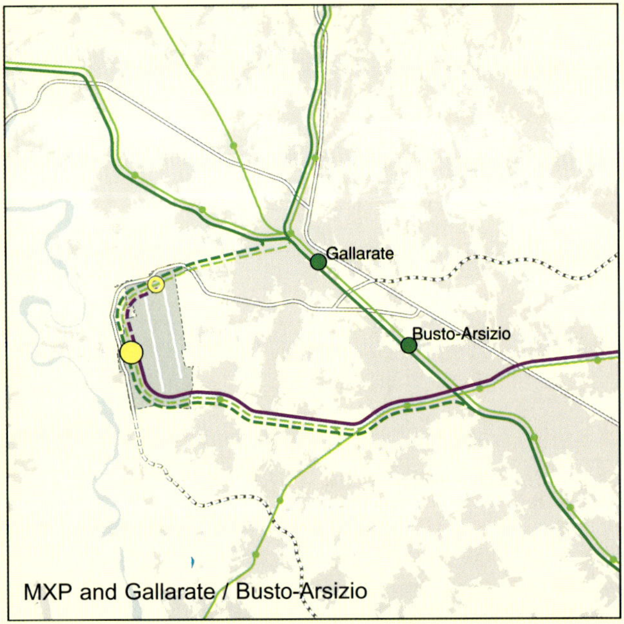
Gallarate
Busto-Arsizio
MXP and Gallarate / Busto-Arsizio

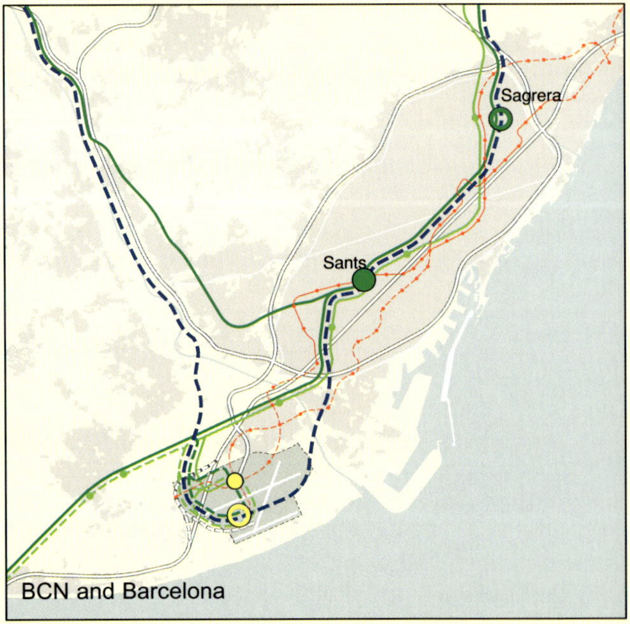
Sagrera
Sants
BCN and Barcelona

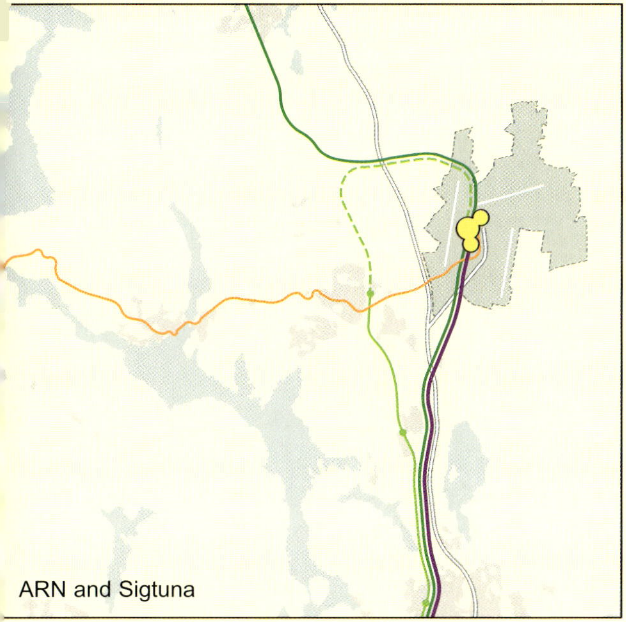
ARN and Sigtuna

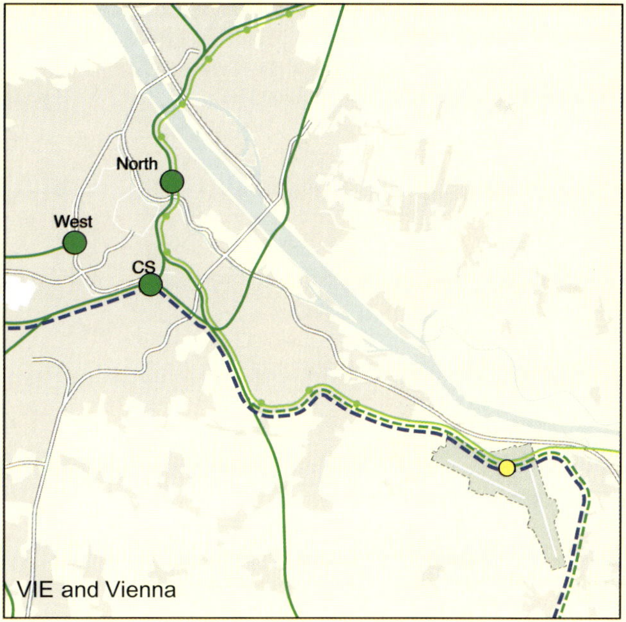
North
West
CS
VIE and Vienna

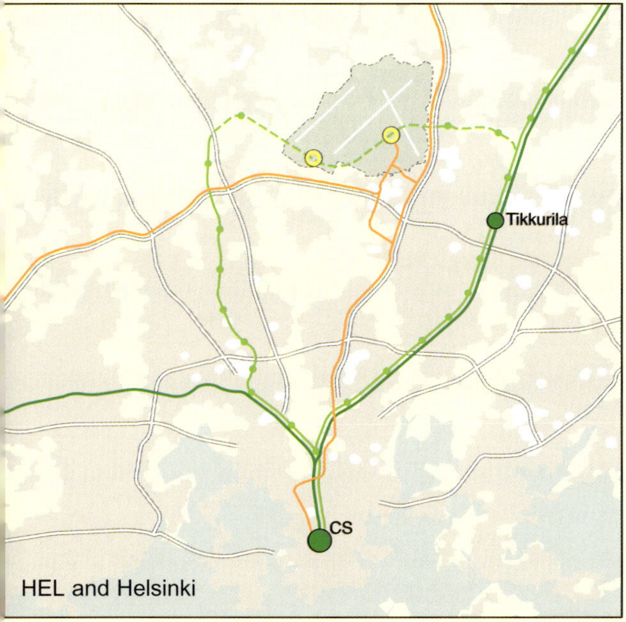
Tikkurila
CS
HEL and Helsinki

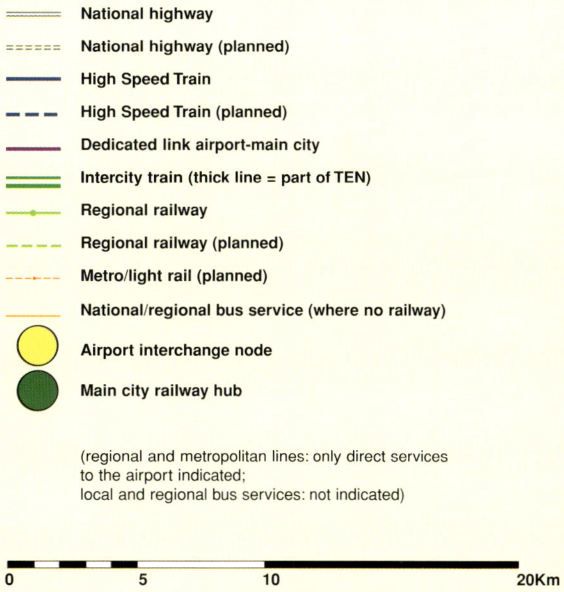
National highway
National highway (planned)
High Speed Train
High Speed Train (planned)
Dedicated link airport-main city
Intercity train (thick line = part of TEN)
Regional railway
Regional railway (planned)
Metro/light rail (planned)
National/regional bus service (where no railway)
Airport interchange node
Main city railway hub
(regional and metropolitan lines: only direct services
to the airport indicated;
local and regional bus services: not indicated)
0
5
10
20Km

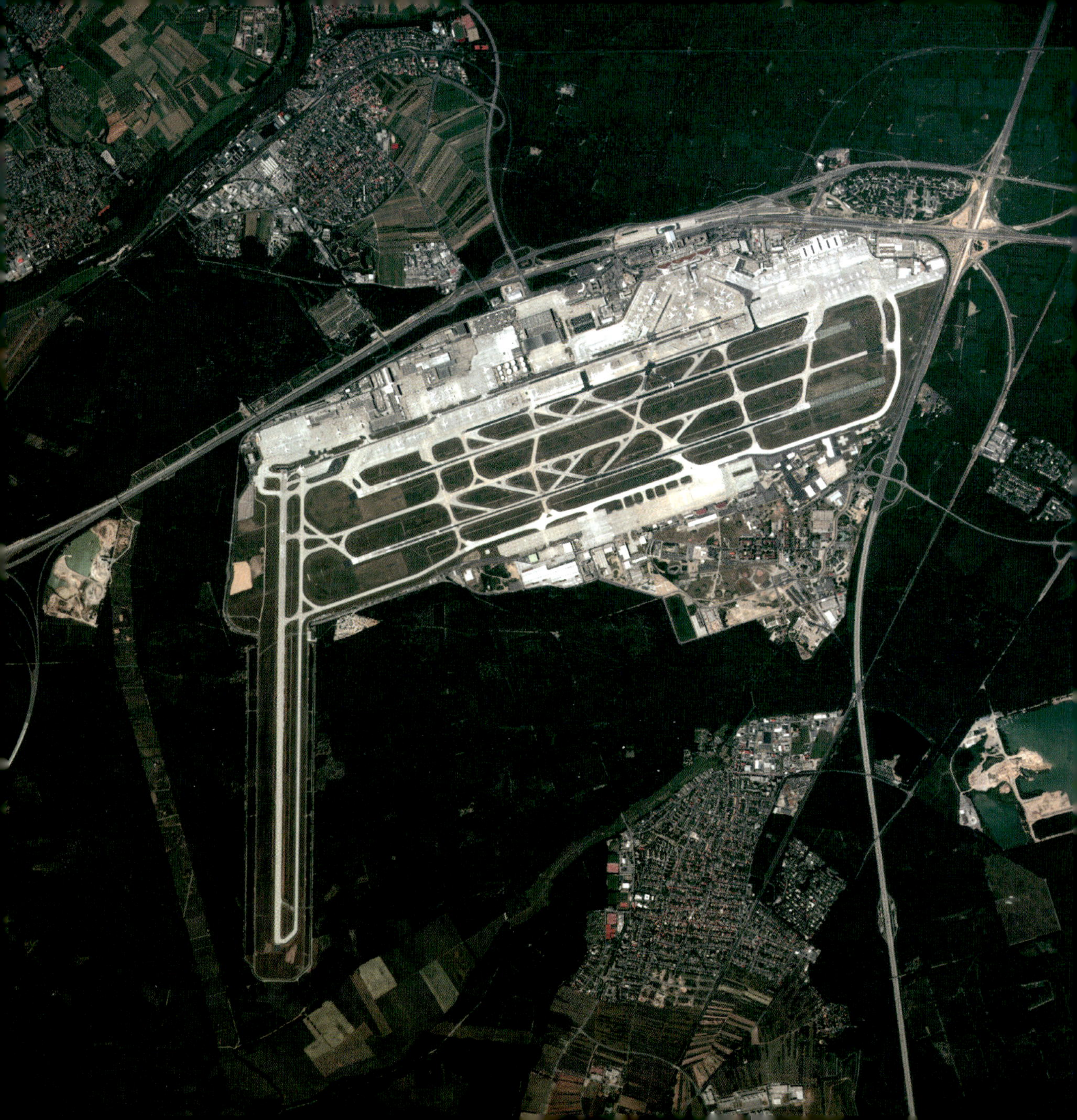

9. Airport interchange

Aerial view

Frankfurt Airport

In many European regions the access roads between city and airport were among the first stretches of highway to be built. The extension of the highway network in subsequent decades led to a major re-orientation in the growth of cities. Today, road and highway access to the airport is in a parlous state, mainly as a result of the general saturation of metropolitan highway networks in the airport area. Due to congestion and its environmental impact, ever-increasing road traffic needs to be replaced by public transport. Due to air space saturation over the major European airports and the environmental impact of air traffic, as many flight movements as possible will have to be diverted onto the HST network. Public transport has accordingly become a strategic tool in airport accessibility. The position and influence of the airport on these networks is likely to rewrite the geography of the region, just as the highways did in their own day.

Not just air passengers

The classic airport railway station has been developed as a satellite of the city's central station, or as an eventual stop on a single railway line. The new airport station is much more than just a station providing access to the terminals. In Zurich, traffic movements to and from the airport that are not generated by air passengers are already over the 60% mark. The airport station has to be made suitable for a wider variety of people, not all of whom are directly related to air traffic. Along with traditional air passengers, these include transfer passengers between High Speed Trains and air, airport and airport city employees, short-time users like consumers, tourists and airport city business clients, and even general commuters or travellers making use of the airport station as a regional landside interchange node. But while the share of public transport of the air passenger segment is still rising, and at many airports reaches levels more typical of inner cities, the share of employees and visitors is usually 10-20% lower.

The facilitation of traffic flows to and from the airport remains the essential task. The common understanding of landside access to airports does not suffice anymore, however. As the contemporary airport is served by High Speed Trains, national railways or coaches, and regional public rail and bus services, transfer between the different modes of landside transport becomes ever more attractive. This has made, and will make, the airport the second main railway station in many regions, and one of the most important stations in the country. With its integration within HST networks, the upcoming interchange function of the airport, and the growth of airport cities, the image of the airport station is changing radically.

Substitution

The European HST network (one of the TEN Trans-European Networks) is being extended, and will directly connect to many continental European airports: the TGV to Paris and Amsterdam, the AVE to Barcelona, the ICE to Berlin and Frankfurt. High Speed Trains offer fast connections between metropolitan regions and it is considered that they will become ever more competitive with air traffic in time and comfort on distances up to 500km.

For the big European airports, integration into this network is a crucial factor, not only for improving competitiveness by enlarging the catchment area, but also for providing an alternative to European "domestic" air traffic. Substitution of short-haul flights is expected to relieve the overcrowded air space and slot tables of the main hub airports, freeing up to 15% of the airport capacity for additional long-haul flights. AMS expects a shift of 5 million air passengers to

Airports are being integrated within the trans-European rail network.

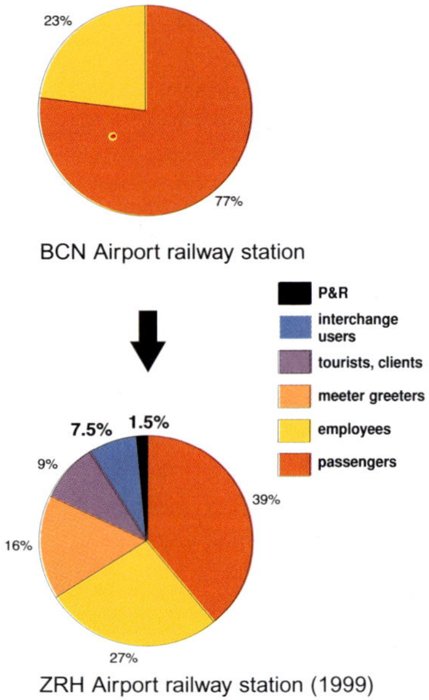

Landside traffic at airports doesn't just mean air passengers: along with 35M passengers a year (or 100,000 per day), 35,000 employees are also there daily. For every three passengers, each one of them making a maximum of one journey to or from the airport, there is one employee making at least two journeys to and from the airport each day. With rising numbers of air transfer passengers, it becomes obvious that employee journeys start to outnumber passenger journeys on public transport. And this is not counting the journeys of visitors and commuters.

integrated airports
non-integrated airports
> 250 km/h
+/- 250 km/h
HEL
HELSINKI
Turku
TALINN
ARN
STOCKHOLM
Norrköping
Pskov
RIGA
Göteborg
Glasgow
Edinburgh
Belfast
DUBLIN
Cork
Liverpool
Manchester
Birmingham
KOBENHAVN
Malmö
Klaipeda
Kaunas
Vilnus
MINSK
Gdansk
Kaliningrad
Hamburg
AMS
AMSTERDAM
LONDON
LGW
Rotterdam
Hannover
BERLIN
Poznan
WARSZAWA
Antw.
Lille
Köln
Leipzig
Dresden
BRUX.
Erfurt
Wroclaw
FRA
LUX.
Metz
PARIS
Mannheim
PRAHA
Katowice
Lvov
Krakow
Nürnberg
Nancy
Strasbourg
Kosice
Uzgorod
WIEN
Bratislava
ZRH
München
VIE
Györ
BUDAPEST
Innsbruck
Lyon
Bolzano
Arad
La Coruña
MXP
Ljubljana
Milano
Verona
Trieste
Craiova
BUCURESTI
Torino
Venezia
BEOGRAD
Bilbao
Dax
Vitoria
Montpellier
Rousse
Porto
Burgos
Lom
Valladolid
Perpignan
Marseille
SOFIA
Zaragoza
Fuentes de O.
Plovdiv
MADRID
Barcelona
SKOPJE
Ormenio
LISBOA
BCN
ROMA
Durres
TIRANE
Thessaloniki
Huelva
Sevilla
ATHINA

the HST by 2005, FRA some 5% of the slot capacity; CDG had already substituted 7.5 million passengers by 2000.
Full integration between air and rail has not yet been achieved, though. DB and Lufthansa have already experimented with joint AiRail services; SNCF and Air France are planning to introduce them too. The necessary co-ordination of the services of both transport systems means not only check-in or luggage-claim facilities in HST stations, but linking the railway station to other terminals as if it were a terminal too. Above all, it means integrated ticketing and streamlined flight and train schedules. The latter seems to be the most urgent task, since the frequency of HST services would have to be fine-tuned to the repetitive waves of arriving and departing aircraft that are typical of the flight plans of hubs.

A second international railway station

High Speed Trains will make two stops in the major European metropolitan areas: at the airport and at the central station. The airport stop will become the point of access to (inter)national rail services for large parts of the region. Many European central railway stations face the handicap of having exploited their spatial reserves: expansion is difficult. A new station at the airport could provide welcome extra capacity, thus solving the problem up to a point.
The question arises, however, as to whether it is possible and sensible to have two "central stations" within one metropolitan area so close to each other. The definition and attribution of complementary roles to the two stations is complex. The interconnection of the HST with regional public transport networks has to be guaranteed, and is therefore usually done downtown. A fully integrated airport station is perceived as a potential competitor to real estate development around the central station itself.

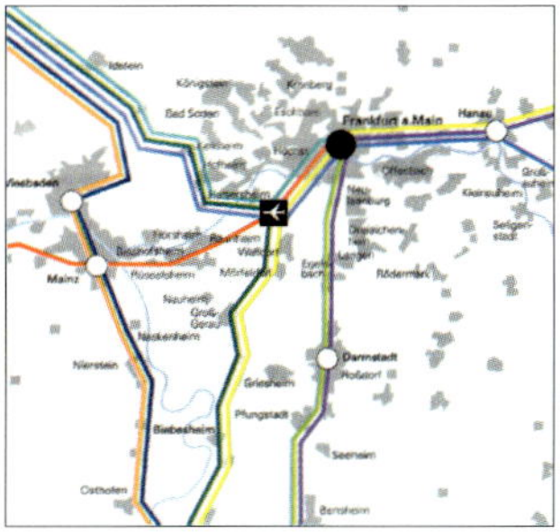

Frankfurt's High Speed Train network: one region —two HST stations.

FRA Dipole

In 1998 Frankfurt Airport, the city, the railways and the regional Public Transport Executive launched a "Dipole Study" to define the respective roles of the two ICE stations for the region, in order to avoid the diverging of the different transport services. With the airport's AIRail terminal, the region has two long-distance railway stations. As in Zurich and Amsterdam, Frankfurt Airport's station is also a second (inter)national interchange between HST services and local/regional networks. Frankfurt anticipates that only two-thirds of all ICE travellers in the AIRail terminal are going to be air passengers. The other third, or approximately 12,000 per day, are expected to be landside interchange users, ICE clients from the region.

So far the central station, the focus of all regional and urban public transport networks, is still the major interchange for (inter)national ICE and IC/EC lines. But it is operating at the limits of its capacity, and currently remains a terminus station, which for the HST means considerable time loss. Given the quality of the airport's AIRail terminal, and its much-frequented regional railway station (230 connections daily), the public authorities wanted to make sure that high-quality access to the city could be preserved, and that the new AIRail terminal would become an "added value" in regional terms. The Dipole Study concluded that the main node of (inter)national HST connection has to remain in the central station. To avoid a shift of long-distance traffic to the airport station, the link between the airport and the central station has to be improved, and travel times minimised. Considerable investment in the central station will be required, in order to transform it into an underground through-station for the ICE, and to add extra capacity.

In view of capacity constraints at Amsterdam Central Station, this city elected a radical forward-looking strategy. The presence of the

Frankfurt Airport's AIRail terminal: a new High Speed Train station underneath a giant platform on top of which 170,000 m^2 *of commercial space will be built.*

Airport interchange

Airport interchange is the airport railway station's function as a node in landside traffic networks: it not only serves air traffic passengers and airport employees, but is also used to interchange between regional and national public transport networks (rail-rail, rail-subway, rail-bus, bus-bus, etc.). It can often provide faster connections to different parts of the region than a central station.

Airport interchange requires the convenient interconnection of all modes of transport. It can be more or less compact in spatial terms. Usually, the railway station concourse is the core of the interchange.

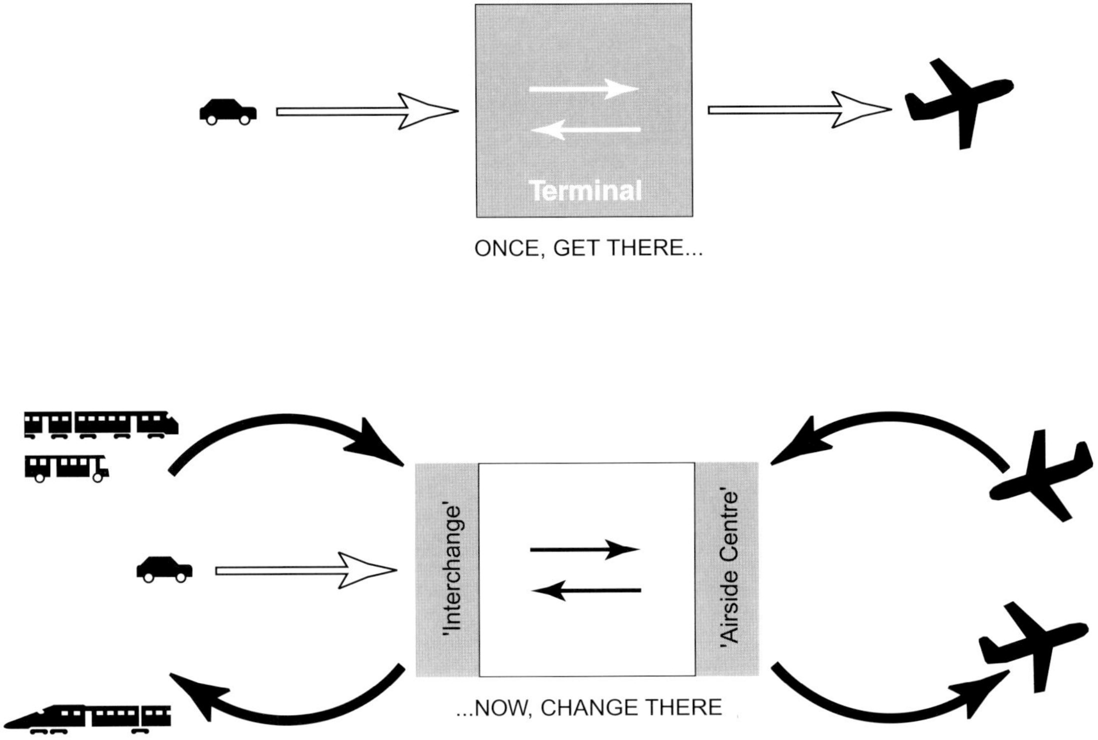

What the hub is on the airside, the interchange node is on the landside. Interchange and airside centres replace "the terminal" as the new centres of the airport.

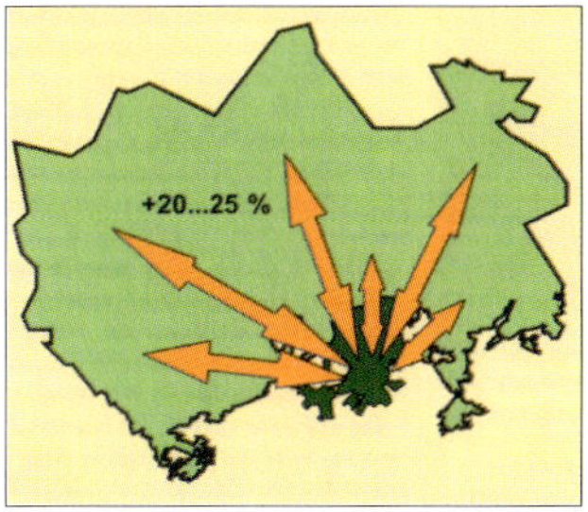

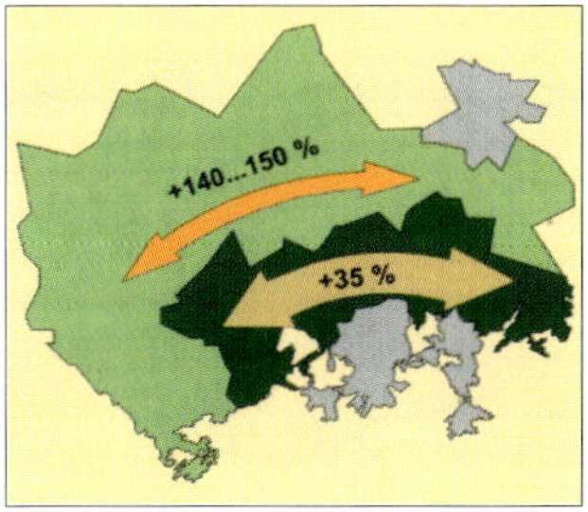

Helsinki: growth of traffic to and from the inner city and of cross-town traffic 1995-2020.

A huge traffic increase (an additional 150%) is expected on the ring roads linking the former peripheral municipalities. As the share of public transport is lower on tangential routes (30% in relation to 51% on the radial routes into Helsinki), investment in them promises to be most effective.

airport and the future HST lines in the region will lead to a complete re-orientation of the city. To avoid a 15-minute detour to the central station, the French TGV and eventually the German ICE will stop in a new southern station on the Zuid-As, with excellent connections to local and urban public transport. Schiphol Airport and this new station will make Amsterdam's former periphery the Netherlands' new international centre, while the old central station will be relegated to being the most important interchange node between regional networks.

With the connection to the HST network, major international airports enhance their function as international gateways to the region. The trans-European HST system will become a large-scale "metro-network" of the club of Euro-regions. Its stations will also acquire a new centrality within their metropolitan region. This marks the definitive end of the era of airports as mere air traffic terminals, and ratifies the urge to refine connections between the airport and other regional centres.

Tangential lines

Once erected on the fringes of urban areas, today's airports reside in heavily urbanised areas, and along some of the most intensively used thoroughfares of the metropolitan region. The capacity of the same roads that provide access to the airport is often exhausted by everyday commuter traffic. The natural increase in traffic movement in the region, and the growth of passenger and commuter traffic to the airport, have a cumulative effect.

At the same time, traffic movements to and from the centre are complemented by an increasing demand for tangential connections between regional centres, including the airport — a traffic segment where the car is still dominant. The regions have to struggle with the fact that regional public transport networks are still very much centre-oriented. They link regional sub-centres —formerly peripheral areas— to the core of the metropolitan area alone. The desire to integrate airports better emerges alongside a commitment to improving tangential public transport links along the periphery of the metropolitan area. Given the precariousness of the situation, initiatives to improve public transport at all levels, and thus to guarantee access for the various users of airports —passengers, employees and visitors— seem to be indispensable.

The twin hub

A look at regional transport plans for the next 10-20 years reveals a surprisingly common pattern in all airport regions. A major part of regional investment in a public transport infrastructure, as well as in road extensions, is concentrated in the airport area. New and planned tangential lines such as Frankfurt's Regionaltangente West (due by 2007), Amsterdam's Zuidtangent (2002), the Stadtbahn Zurich (2005), Vienna's S-Bahn 9 (2003), and Helsinki's Marja-line (after 2011) all run via the airport. With so much investment being put into public transport and into improved services, it becomes increasingly attractive to use the airport station as a landside interchange for non-air passengers. The airport railway station is a welcome opportunity to interconnect these new lines with existing rail services, and thus to improve regional public transport in general.
This definitively marks the strategic position of the airport station within the regional transport network. What the hub airport is to the airside, the multi-modal interchange becomes to the landside. The same principle that makes an airport a hub makes an airport railway station a regional hub: when a critical mass is reached through transfer passengers, more connections and a higher fre-

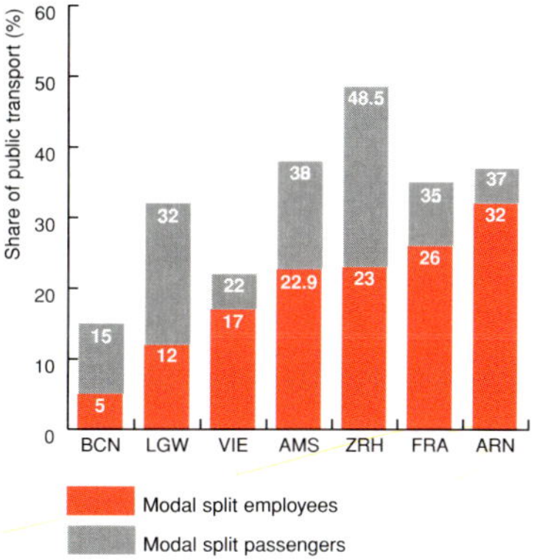

The share of public transport for employees is considerably lower than that of passengers.

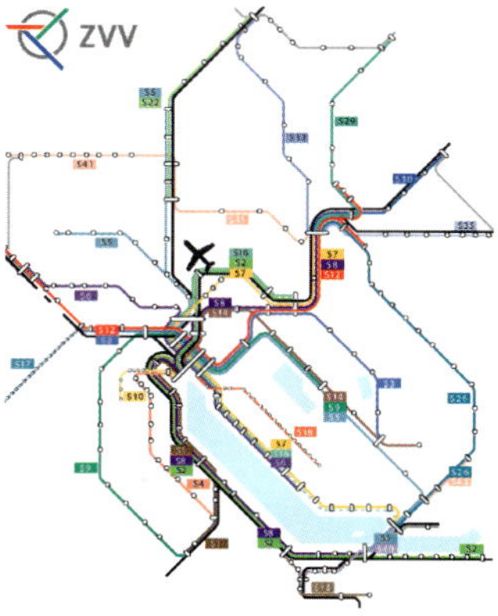

Zurich's S-Bahn network: consolidating a regional interchange at the airport.

quency in services can be offered. The repercussions on the modal split to the airport, particularly of employees' traffic, will be considerable. This is all the more important, given that the modal split in traffic to the airport has often remained below the average of regional centres.

The interchange: a political issue, or not?

In the Zurich, Amsterdam and Frankfurt regions, and even in the relatively remote Gatwick, the airport is already one of the top multimodal regional interchange nodes. With the sole exception of Zurich Airport station, there is as yet no quantitative evaluation of this function, however. The airport station is used as an interchange, but this is not yet part of official policy. Regional transport strategies usually continue focussing on the provision of simple "connections" to the airport. Providing "interconnections" at the airport, and perceiving the airport as a node in a network, is not yet standard practice. Interchanging remains a welcome by-product, with the consequence that only part of the transport potential generated by the enormous investment in landside accessibility for airports is actually exploited.

In terms of quality, however, an evaluation seems possible. Interchanging at the airport often offers faster and more convenient connections than the detour via a central station, thus making the airport station itself attractive for commuters to and from the region. An interchange at the airport allows for accessing areas of a region which are as yet remote, and therefore poorly served via the centre.

At Gatwick Airport, fast rail links to London are very efficient, but local public transport is underdeveloped. As a consequence, the opportunity to interchange at the airport largely consists of a commuters' "Park & Ride" scheme. P & R occupies a large part of the airport's parking places, notwithstanding the considerable parking fees. But given Gatwick's 45,000 parking places —as compared to Schiphol's 18,000, or Frankfurt Airport's 17,000— there are no severe constraints to parking opportunities for employees and passengers.

Usually, however, interchanging in the form of P & R is not desired at airports. It may only become an interesting concept by linking car to HST travel. As in most regions, Schiphol Airport's HST station is directly accessible from the highway network, while the city's central station is not. It is not in vain, then, that the HST is promoted as if it were an aviation service. The substituting of short-haul air traffic will increase this notion of the interchange.

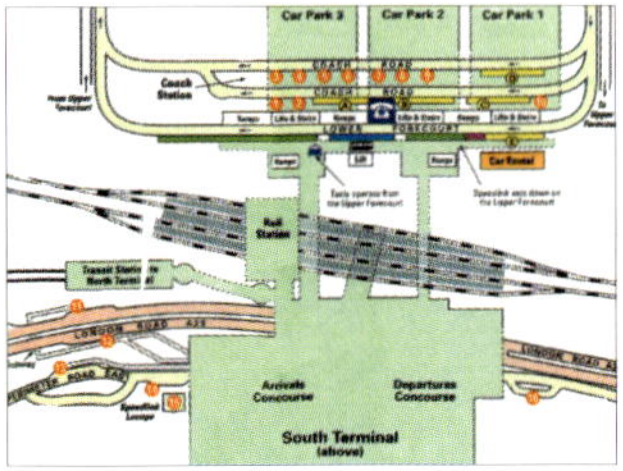

At Gatwick Airport commuters need to enter and pass through the air terminal to get from bus or car to the railway platforms, and vice-versa. The investment required to improve the quality of public transport provision and interconnection would, in the eyes of BAA Gatwick and Railtrack (the operator of the train station), as well as the other public transport providers (all private), only be justified in conjunction with real estate development around the node, however.

The airport railway station

The fact that there is as yet no policy regarding their interchange function is a strong drawback vis-à-vis the organisational quality of most airport stations. Inter-modality usually focuses on AiRail interchange alone. Interconnections are still considered from the perspective of the air terminals, and have not yet been rendered suitable for switching between trains and buses. It is no longer sufficient to simply connect each mode to the air terminals. The efficiency of the interchange function depends on the quality of the interconnection between the different modes of transport. Financial involvement on the part of the airport operator will be necessary to guarantee this.

In Zurich Airport's current fifth phase of expansion —probably for the first time in airport history— a similar amount of capital is invested in improving the landside interchange (300 million Euros) as in a completely new 27-gate terminal building, the midfield dock

(300 million), or in the airside centre (260 million). This major effort is being undertaken to establish direct and convenient connections within the station building between all landside modes. The airport operator, the home carrier and the Swiss Federal Railways are working together on the extension and radical upgrading of the station concourse in order to integrate all public transport resources at the airport, while at the same time establishing air traffic-related services such as check-in and baggage claim in the railway station. These new facilities will make Zurich Airport a linchpin in the public transport system for north Zurich and the surrounding region.

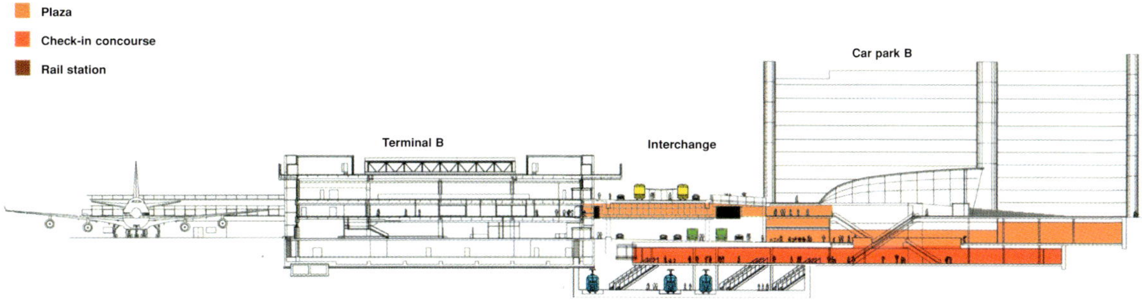

Zurich Airport rail station —a landside interchange in the making. Already 9% of all rail passengers are pure "interchangers" between different train services.

In contrast to Zurich, the absence of an equivalent combined effort between rail and bus operators at Gatwick is the main reason for the lack of interchange quality there. The breaking up of British Rail, along with its privatisation, has resulted in no less than six independent rail companies serving Gatwick. This and the great variety of coach services next door make co-ordination of the interchange function particularly difficult, both in terms of direct access between the different services, and scheduling. Added to which, the restrictions on land use development on the airport platform and its immediate surroundings undermine the realisation of a quality landside interchange. Both the BAA and the public transport operators are reluctant to create an interchange without getting the chance to exploit it in terms of real estate development. The question must be raised as to whether an interchange, and interchange quality, depend on an economically profitable airport city.

The location factor

In comparison to other poles in the metropolitan area, the airport is one of the most accessible public transport nodes. This trend is not to be underestimated. For its three new HST stations and their environs, Barcelona has worked out different and very particular development concepts. This also means different functions for these stations in the future. The present central station function at Sants Station is being consolidated along with its urban significance. Sagrera, the most important HST station, will be the core of a new urban centre and a catalyst to the redevelopment of a long-neglected district. The airport station is part of the "Plan Delta" scheme, a strategy making the delta of the River Llobregat the metropolitan area's logistical platform with a seaport, airport, industry, and freight distribution nodes and networks.

The accessibility of airports will greatly improve in the future. Enormous pre-investment in landside accessibility has been undertaken, mostly to expand the air traffic function. Now it is crucial to anticipate the potential added value such a multi-modal interchange can have for the further development of the metropolitan area. Any place a lot of people pass through is where tremendous opportunities for business exist. Multi-modal connections at all levels, from the local to the international, tend to trigger urban development around and directly on the territory of the airport. And as the regional and international traffic interfaces of entire European regions, airports are very attractive to business development, not only on the platform but also beyond it. Local and regional authorities urgently need to understand the major potential around this transport node, and to carefully evaluate the airport's role as a regional development pole.

10. Opportunities in the airport area

Aerial view

Milan-Malpensa Airport

The size of a city

Airport cities are built very quickly. Growth rates (the amount of new floor area erected) in the 1990s were literally proportional to the growth rates in air traffic. This boom is not only propelled by logistical activities or by airport services directly related to the air traffic industry. An increasing number of enterprises which were formerly located in town centres or peripheral business parks are attracted by the image of the airport location and the good connections offered there. In the more advanced cases, a variegated, heterogeneous complex of activities settles around the airport, reflecting the increased value of the land.

A major airport renders the surrounding land into something that is highly desirable. Along with global air connections, it is their strategic position within landside infrastructural networks that has made airport surroundings one of the most attractive business locations in the city periphery. In terms of size and complexity of organisation, the airport area becomes comparable to a city.

The attitudes of airport municipalities with respect to their airport are ambivalent. The airport has undoubtedly become the cornerstone of many local and regional economies. Northern Holland hopes, in view of the end of the boom of the 1990s, to be able to stabilise or even re-launch its economy with anti-cyclic investment in Schiphol Airport as the seemingly most dynamic pillar of the region's economy.

In contrast, Crawley and the other municipalities within the Gatwick Airport area, an economically thriving zone which in 2000 had an unemployment rate of virtually 0%, want to diversify their economic structure in order to depend less on the air traffic industry and its unpredictable fluctuations. The downturn in the air traffic industry during the Gulf War hit the airport area particularly

The airport area is in the crossfire of differing ambitions:

Airport operators seek to attract activities that complement their operations, either functionally or financially. They therefore set up comprehensive strategies encompassing airport operation and business development, even beyond their platform.

Local authorities wish for planning security. They have to deal with all the nuisances from air traffic and congestion on their roads, which can be significantly harmful to their own interests. However, they are often inclined to go after their own share of the development spin-off from the airport's image.

Regional (and national) authorities seek to guarantee the airport's operability, while minimising environmental impacts. They mean to guide the development of potential airport cities in a way that does not adversely affect other regional poles. Urban development will have to be concentrated on sites with high, preferably multi-modal, accessibility.

Investors and developers (including airport subsidiaries) demand both clarity and development security in order to willingly make investments, along the lines of “when, where, how much?” They require guaranteed site conditions, including accessibility in general, and access to the airport.

Future tenants demand an ever-higher environmental quality. Proximity to the airport alone is no longer a sufficiently strong argument.

Transport providers —airlines as well as landside transport operators— seek to optimise their services, including joint ventures to exploit synergies (e.g. AiRail) and to enhance inter-modality. In exchange for high pre-investment in infrastructures, they demand a share in the development opportunities these create through their services, such as the exploitation of shops inside the airport station.

hard. Too much regional activity was related to the operation of Gatwick Airport, the main generator of local employment by far: hotels, distribution and catering, transport and communications, and business services.

Opportunities

In spite of this ambivalence, a growing airport means, for most airport municipalities, commercial opportunities that compensate for such increasing constraints as noise, further limitations to housing development, or traffic congestion on access roads. With the enormous market demand of the 1990s, they have speeded up their own competing development plans, mainly along their access infrastructures. In order to profit from rising land prices around the airport, they have launched their own airport business parks and airport centres, or "aerovilles". Kelsterbach and Walldorf in Frankfurt provide logistical parks, and Opfikon-Glattbrugg at Zurich Airport offers, among other things, a housing and business location that, with its 7,500 employees and 6,000 inhabitants, amounts to almost 50% of the entire municipality. At Schiphol —a former dormitory town for Amsterdam— the airport municipality is developing, in exclusivity, an enormous business park of 350,000 m^2 just south of the platform.

Most of these projects are carried out by developers who have managed to acquire land around the airport, such developments being welcomed by regional authorities. Co-ordination across several municipalities is difficult, if not neglected, not least because such projects often exceed the scale of what smaller municipalities are accustomed to handling. The temptation to go on converting more agricultural land in response to new market demands is high. In such instances, there is not much control over whether what is devel-

Amsterdam
Schiphol
AMSTERDAM CITY CENTER
AMSTELVEEN
HOOFDDORP
TELEPORT
SOUTH AXIS
AMSTERDAM AIRPORT AREA

oped has a direct relation to air traffic. Such fragmented initiatives are likely to further increase the disparity between both the quality and capacity of access networks and the speed of economic growth in the airport area.

In terms of the size and complexity of its organisation, the airport area becomes comparable to the city.

Off-airport

Until recently it was still unthinkable for airport operators to appear as (private) developers beyond the confines of their own platform. Now it is becoming ever more common. Obviously, they try to accommodate a major share of valuable business and service activities (airport-oriented ones) on their own territory. As space on the platform is scarce, however, their own land and real estate development companies become more aggressive and search for investment opportunities outside the restricted platform. This is not just for operational flexibility alone —as were out-sourced airline administrations or catering— but in order to receive extra revenue by participating in real estate projects in the airport surroundings.
Vienna Airport plc has created a "Vienna Airport Business Park" development company, to develop an off-airport site with some 140,000 m^2 of office floor space. Frankfurt Airport, Europe's no. 1 air freight hub, is eager to provide a more substantial package of surfaces for logistics and distribution, which it can no longer accommodate on its own platform. And so Fraport co-operates with the Hoechst Company in the promotion of a former industrial area for logistics. Along with its branch Schiphol Real Estate (SRE), Schiphol Airport participates not only in the development of a 300 ha logistical area called "A4-Zone" just outside its platform, but also promotes and commissions business parks close to various Dutch regional airports, in partnership with their respective municipalities.

A powerful foreign player

The most extreme example of such off-airport real estate development can currently be witnessed around Malpensa Airport. Its initiator is, however, not the SEA, operator of the various Milan airports, but the recently set up Malpensa Real Estate plc, a non-Italian company with a 60% share held by Schiphol's SRE. Together with its local partners, this company is developing an area for logistical businesses —with two more in the pipeline— plus an office park in the wider airport area. SRE has thereby filled the development vacuum that appeared after the overwhelming rise in air traffic at Malpensa, the airport moving from 6 to 21 million passengers in a short space of time. The airport municipalities —who are hidebound by strong political rivalry with each other— were unable to respond quickly enough to the unexpected opportunities.

A foreign player gets involved in the making of Milan-Malpensa's airport city. Between the River Ticino and the terminals of Malpensa Airport, Malpensa Real Estate —an SRE subsidiary— joins in on the airport's own business park (1) and plans to develop an airport city strip with a "trade park" of 55,000 m² (2), the redevelopment of parts of Vizzola Ticino (3), and a golf course (4).

Airports like Schiphol are ever more experienced in developing land for activities that, for whatever reason, need to be close to the airport. With them exporting this expertise and getting globally involved in developing airport cities, another very adroit player is introduced into the arena. Since such potential partners in real estate development are no longer regional or national operators, local authorities yet again face completely different conditions in terms of co-operation.

Regeneration of the metropolitan area

The latest airport operator initiatives are met with suspicion by local and regional authorities, who claim that an airport operator ought to run an airport, not develop the land around it. Spontaneous initiatives by local authorities, in turn, are opposed by

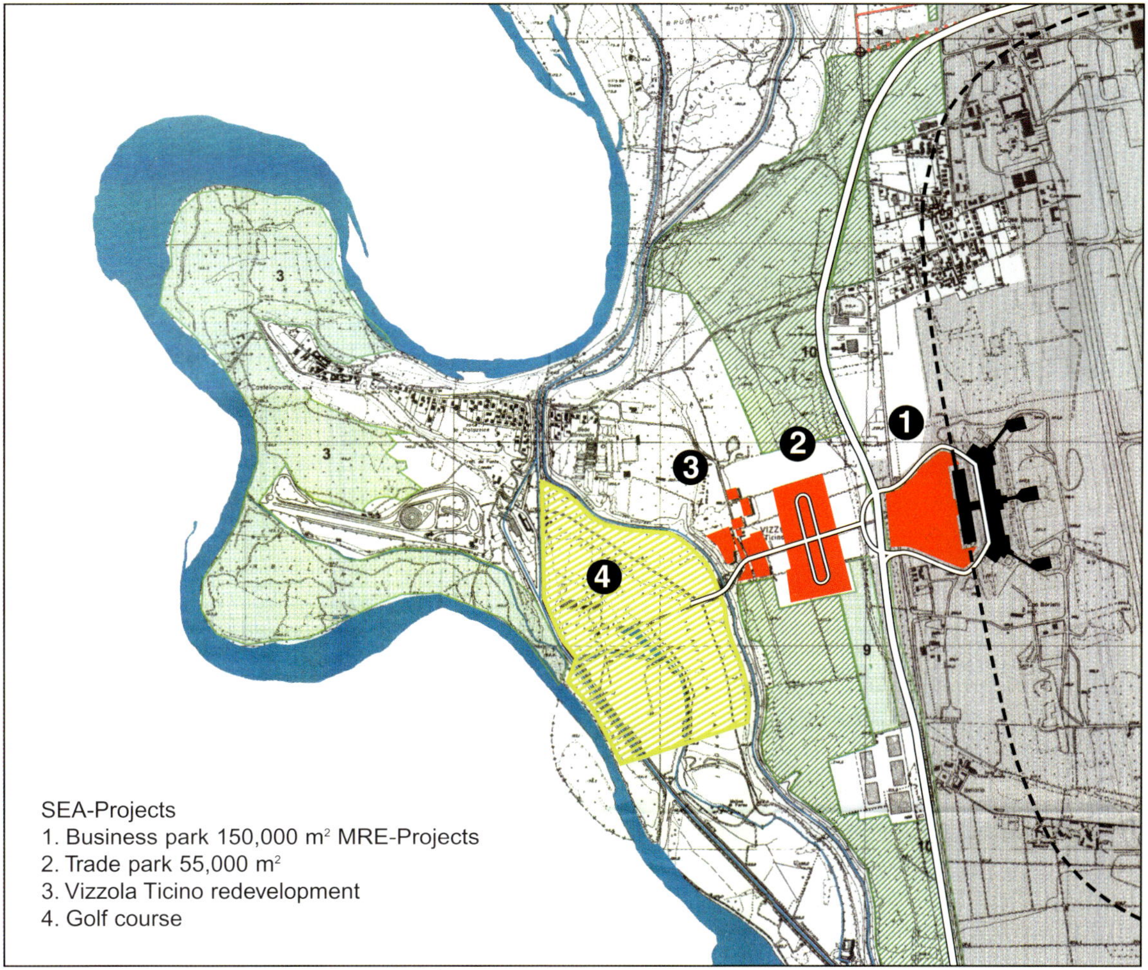
SEA-Projects
1. Business park 150,000 m² MRE-Projects
2. Trade park 55,000 m²
3. Vizzola Ticino redevelopment
4. Golf course

airport operators who fear for the elasticity and manoeuvrability of the airport in the long-term.

To limit the focus to the immediate airport vicinity would be too narrow a view. International airports have become major assets for the respective regional economies. The benefits of an expanding airport are disbursed over a larger area. Particularly in regions where traffic connections to the airport are good, the spin-off from the latter does not necessarily have to be concentrated around the platform, but can also be accommodated in dispersed sites throughout the region, thus contributing to a potentially more judicious distribution of benefits.

If access to the airport can be guaranteed, it becomes possible to settle closer to the city. At fifteen minutes road and rail distance from the airport, the booming northern periphery of Stockholm is the preferred location of IT and high-tech businesses in the region. These kinds of business are predisposed to international relations and thus to air traffic, but above all they seek proximity to a city. In Zurich the fact that the central station can be reached 150 times a day, and is only ten minutes away from the airport, makes the redevelopment around the former extremely competitive vis-à-vis any other site that is physically closer to the airport: it is door-to-door with the terminals. A remote green-field airport like Munich, on the other hand, reveals a massive concentration of activities around the platform. There is little economic impact beyond its immediate surroundings, due to poor network integration.

Good access to the highway infrastructure, as well as to metropolitan and regional public transport systems, allows other more remote areas to be reconsidered for development. This criterion applies particularly to airport-related activities such as logistics and distribution: direct access to the platform, freight handlers and ter-

SADC AMS

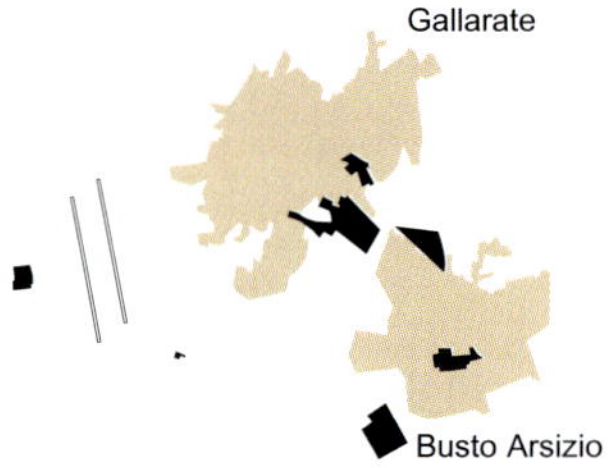

MXP Area Plan

Two regions, two concepts: concentration or spreading of airport-related activities.

minals is more important than spatial contiguity. Since their corporate image and operation are less sensitive to remote locations, such activities can be situated as much as 30-40 km from the airport. BAA Gatwick, for example, considers it possible to move them to towns along the south coast, an area in strong need of regeneration.

Who or what wishes to be at the airport is not always who or what really needs to be there. The right balance must be found between concentrating a certain kind of programme close to the airport and distributing other airport-related programmes in the wider surroundings.

Such a regional development concept —an approach mainly favoured by regional and less strategically positioned local authorities— needs a lot of steering, however, much more so than that required by spontaneous accommodation right next to the airport. There are clear discrepancies in the development opportunities between airport and regional sites. Sites on or around airports can often be developed much faster. Sites closer to and in the city — especially redevelopment locations— require more pre-investment and more complex development co-operation. But this approach is likely to generate less conflict and bottlenecks in the long term.

Piano territoriale d'Area Malpensa

The Lombardy region has developed one of the more solid strategies thus far for replacing "opportunism" by "orchestration" in the airport area: the "Piano territoriale d'Area Malpensa". The Malpensa area needs redevelopment, not new development. Due to recent economic decline in the traditional manufacturing industries (textiles and mechanical engineering), the municipalities around

Malpensa are left with huge stocks of brown-field sites. To overcome this decline, they have launched a number of independent rehabilitation operations, creating a wide range of development sites in the region. On top of that, most of their plans for new housing development have become impossible, due to the airport's growing noise impact.

These towns see an accumulation of airport-related activities around Malpensa as a chance to stimulate regeneration of their own brown-field sites at some 10-15 km to the east of the airport. The main task of the "Piano d'Area Malpensa" has been to establish structures for local co-operation in the development of the Malpensa area and to compensate for insecurities about the future growth of Malpensa Airport. On the basis of an extraordinary overview of all ongoing planning initiatives, it proposes to distribute as much as possible of the airport's potential spin-off. Development on new sites in and around the airport is to be minimised, while re-use of the former industrial areas available within the limits of the surrounding towns —such as Gallarate and Busto-Arsizio— is to be stimulated to the maximum. The sites near the airport are to be reserved for a limited amount of specifically airport-related functions: the "Cargo City", as well as hotel and conference facilities. The "Piano d'Area" promotes "a co-ordinated and controlled growth of complementary, multifunctional development poles".

Such a diffusion of the economic impact of Malpensa Airport will require reconsideration of the accessibility of the Malpensa area. The potential axes of urban development, towards Gallarate and the south, have yet to be equipped with adequate means of public transport.

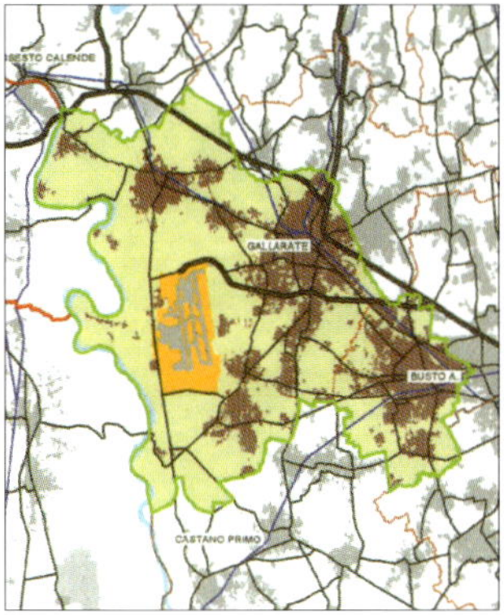

Perimeter of the "Piano d'Area Malpensa": With the shift of operations from Milan Linate to Malpensa Airport in October 1998, this new north-Italian hub grew from 6M passengers to 21M in just two years. Its success outstripped every forecast and has put increasing pressure on the local planning context. Anticipating the challenge to integrate this huge airport in the territory, the "Piano territoriale d'Area Malpensa" was produced in 1999. It sets up a framework for co-ordinated action between the region, 3 provinces, the airport operator, and a group of 17 municipalities directly affected by the development of the airport. The "Piano d'Area" is no binding plan. It depends absolutely on the participation of the dozens of mayors involved, and on future possibilities to implement and monitor this process.

Development sites

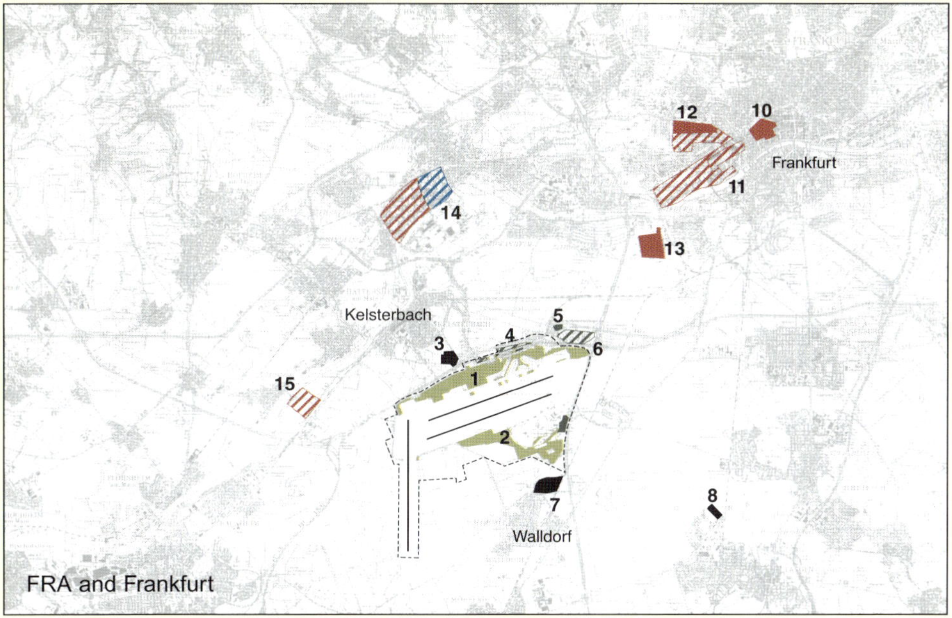

1 Airport terminal area, Cargo City North
2 Cargo City South
3 Kelsterbach Trade Port
4 AIRail Terminal - Business Center hotel, commerce, offices, medical care center, 170'000 m²
5 Hotel
6 Gateway Gardens future airport-related activities
7 Walldorf industrial area logistics and other airport related activities
8 Airtraffic Control Germany (DFS) administration
10 Frankfurt's central financial district
11 Frankfurt Main Station: "Frankfurt 21" - redevelopment
12 Frankfurt Fairgrounds redevelopment
13 Niederrad Office Park
14 Former Hoechst Industries redevelopmet, partly for airport related activities
15 Former Caltex refinery redevelopment

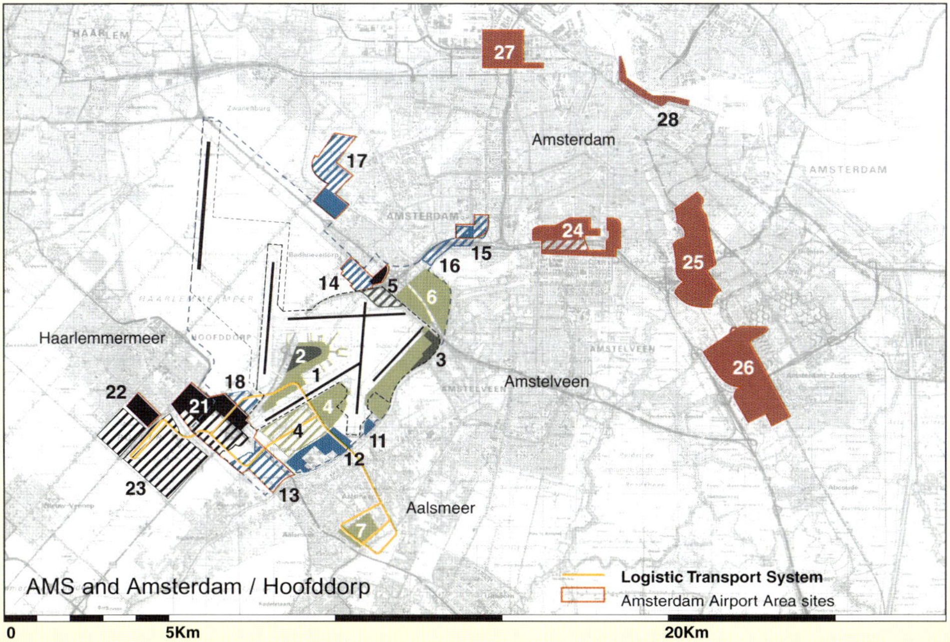

1 Schiphol Centre / Schiphol South terminals, cargo
2 Schiphol Centre - AirportCity offices and hotels, 200,000 m²
3 Schiphol East new office / company park, 125,000 m²
4 Schiphol SouthEast new cargo centre, 100,000 m²
5 Schipohl Elzenhof offices (incl. EHQ), 180,000 m²
6 Schiphol Golf and business centre
7 Alsmeer Flower Auction (EU's Nr.1)
11 Sky Park logistics (1/3 offices), 24,000 m²
12 Schiphol Rijk logistics / offices (50/50), 35 ha
13 Schiphol Logistics Park logistics / offices, 130 ha
14 Badhoevendorp South logistics, 30 ha
15 Riekerpolder International Business Park Nissan, IBM, offices, 160,000 m²
16 Oude Haagse Weg future logistics, 6 ha
17 Lijnden/Lutkemeer logistics, 65 ha
18 De Hoek
21 Beukenhorst (Haarlemmermeer) business park, (44 ha reserve)
22 The President (Haarlemmermeer) companies / logistics, 30 ha
23 Grondbank A4 (H'meer, SRE, KLM)
24 Amsterdam Zuid-As 650,000 m² offices, 6,000 apartments, 160,000 m² commerce / entertainment
25 Amsterdam Amstel III
26 Amsterdam Zuid-Oost
27 Amsterdam Teleport
28 IJ Oevers

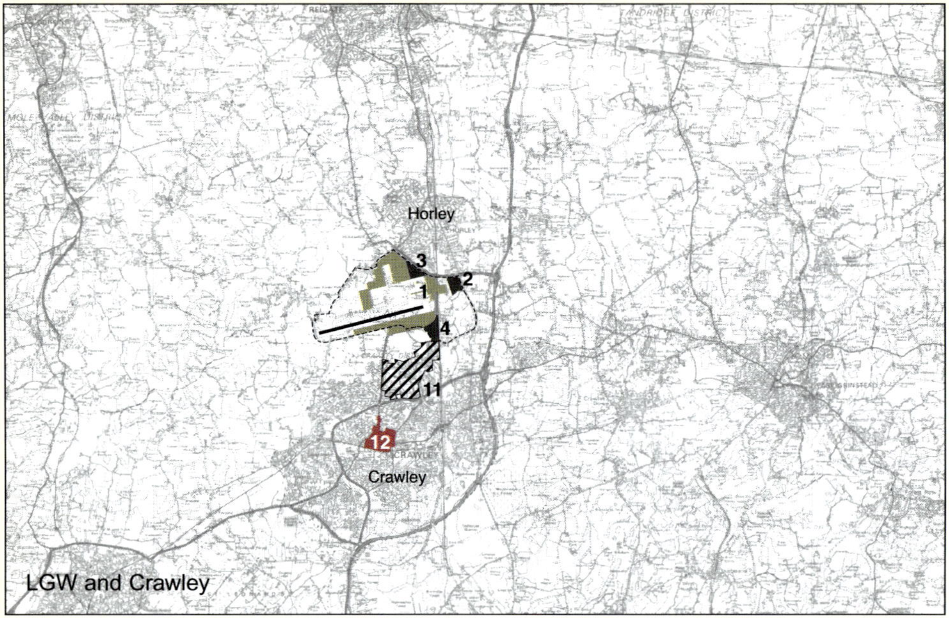

1 Operational area
terminals, cargo, maintenance
2 Platform hotel area 1
3 Platform hotel area 2
4 BAA Beehive site
offices, 55,000 m²
11 Manor Royal Estate
business park (IT etc.)
12 Crawley Town Centre
commerce, business

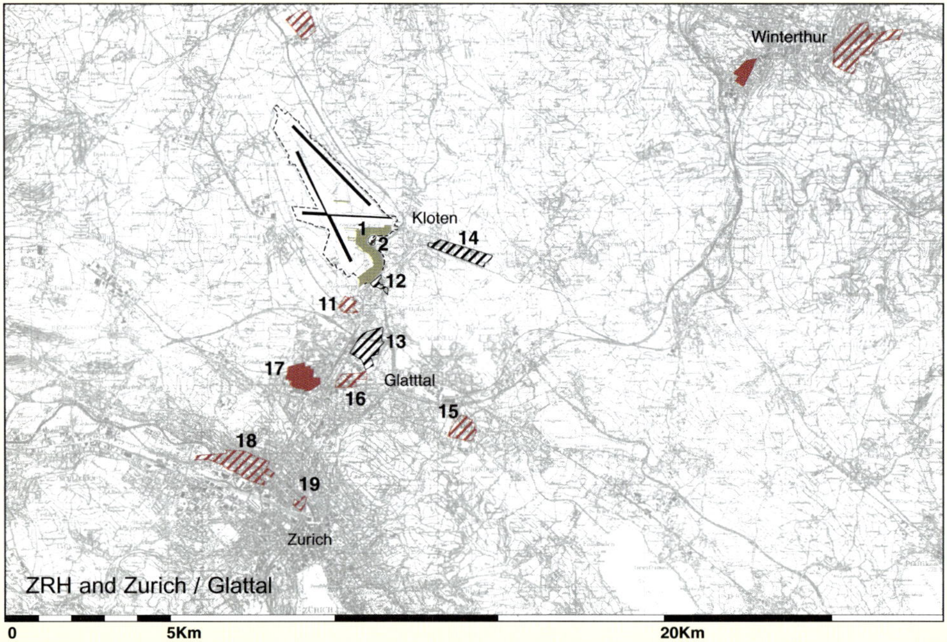

1 Operational area
terminals, maintenance, cargo
2 Butzenbuehl area
offices, 120,000 m²
11 Cher
back-up offices
12 Balsberg
shopping mall, multipurpose stadium
13 Oberhauserriet
urban and residential district, 60 ha
6,000 inhabitants, 20-30,000 workplaces
14 Kloten industrial area
outsourced airport functions, logistics
15 Hochbord Duebendorf
shopping, sports, industry, offices
16 Leutschenbach TV Studio, WTC
urban and residential district, hotels, offices
17 Zurich Nord urban redevelopment
hotel, fair, stadium, tertiary, 71 ha
18 Zurich West urban redevelopment
hotels, theatre, industry, soccer stadium,
service, residential, 67-90 ha
19 HB Southwest Zurich main railway station
area redevelopment with housing, offices,
commerce

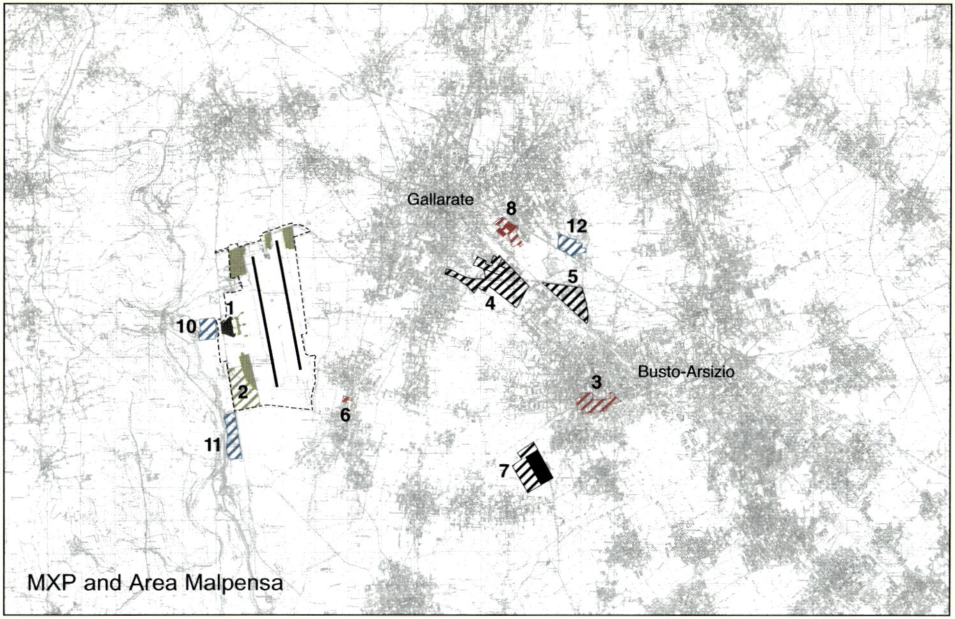

1 Malpensa Business Park
offices, hotel, 150,000m^2
2 Cargo City / Zona Franca
logistics, showrooms, offices, 8,000 m^2
3 Busto Arsizio Business Park
offices, services, housing, 302,000 m^2
4 Gallarate Special Development Zone
university, exhibition centre, housing, entertainment, 160,000 m^2
5 Gallarate Inter-modal Freight Terminal (HUPAC), 330,000 m^2
6 Ferno-Lonate Pozzolo Station area redevelopment: 19,000 m^2
7 Busto Arsizio industrial zone
950,000 m^2
8 Gallarate new industrial zone
350,000 m^2
10 Vizzola Ticino Trade Centre
offices, hotel, showrooms, 52,000 m^2
11 Malpensa Logistics Park
offices, warehouses, 50,000m^2
12 Gallarate Business Park
offices 20,000m^2

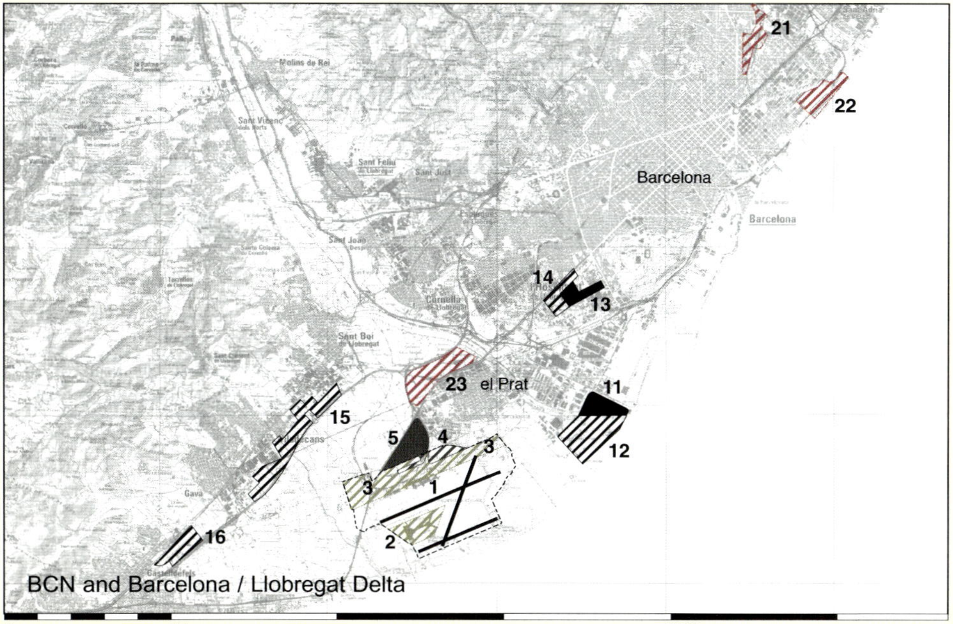

1 Airport: operational area today
2 Airport: new terminal area
3 Airport: operational planned
4 Airport: tertiary developments planned
Total airport:
30,000-40,000 employees forecast
208 ha, 798,000 m^2
5 Mas Blau I and II
business park, 33 ha
11 ZAL Logistic Activities Zone today
80 ha, 370,000 m^2
12 ZAL Logistic Activities Zone extension
120 ha, 550,000 m^2
13 New trade-fair enclosure
15 ha, 117,000 m^2
14 Logistics park
15 Logistics park
16 Logistics park
21 Sagrera Station surroundings
commercial, business, housing
55 ha, 750,000 m^2
22 Diagonal Mar
commercial, business
46 ha, 627,000 m^2
23 El Prat urban development
housing, commercial, business

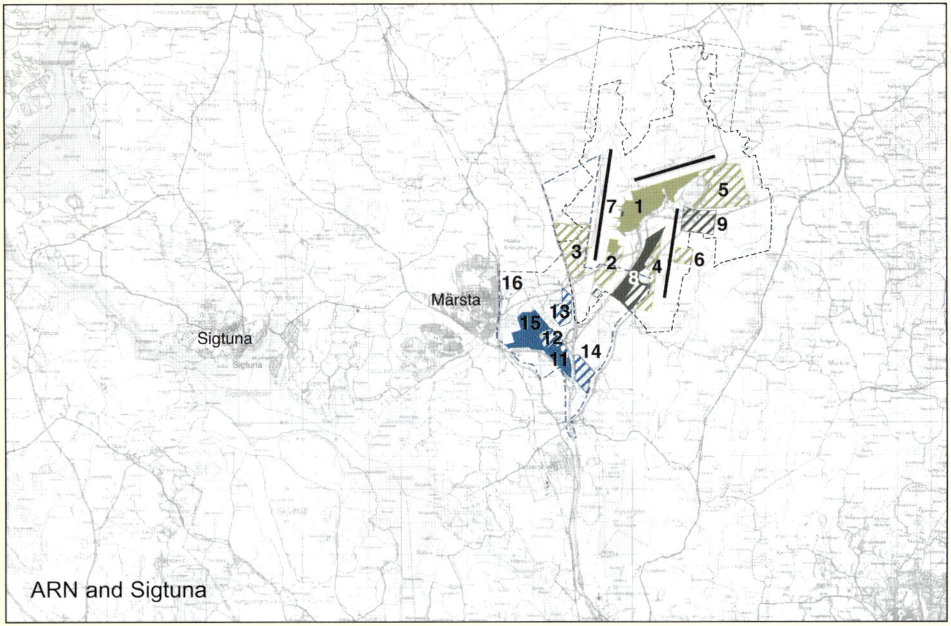

1 Operational area
terminal and service area
2 Freight area 1
3 Arlanda Logistic Centre
Freight area 2
4 Service area
5 Extended hangar area
6 Service area
7 SkyCity
business, conference, hotel, 77,000 m²
8 Airport City on platform
land-use to be intensified
9 Trade-fair enclosure
11 Arlandastad - Block 1
Eurostop Hotel and shopping
12 Arlandastad - Block 2
logistics park, 200,000 m²
(1st phase of North European Logistic and Hi-tech Centre)
13 Arlandastad - Block 3
logistics: extension of 12
14 Arlandastad - Block 4
office park and hotel, 170,000 m²
15 Brista business and light-industrial park
16 Original perimeter of Arlandastad
593 ha

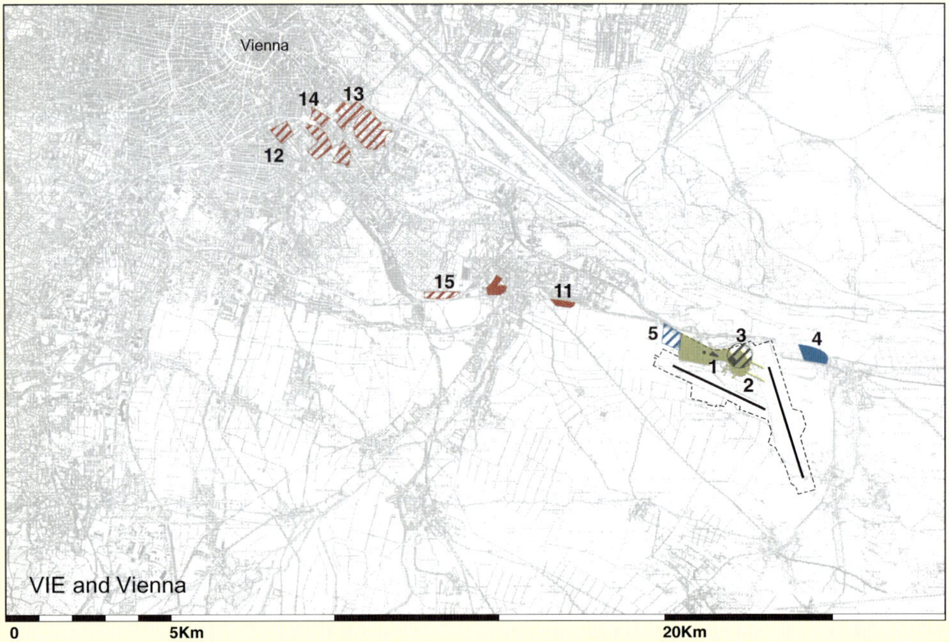

1 Operational area
2 World Trade Centre, hotels
3 Office park (planned)
offices, 12,000 m² (until 2002)
4 Vienna Airport business park
business and logistics, 140,000 m²
5 Messenger and Express Centre
11 Concorde Business Park, Schwechat
offices, 49,000 m²
12 New Vienna Central Station
13 Erdberger Mais, gasometer area;
former abattoir
urban redevelopment, 200 ha
14 Aspanggruende
urban redevelopment, 22 ha
15 Business park Ailecgasse

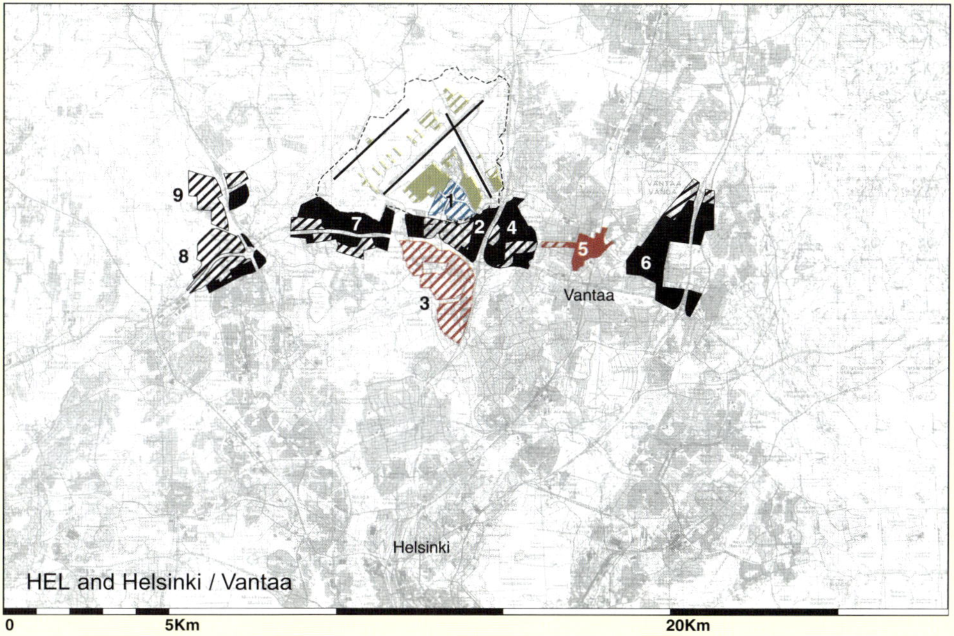

1 Aviapolis (Airport City)
offices, logistics
2 Veromies / tertiary
offices and hotels
3 Pakkala-Tammisto
mixed programme, perishables, large-scale retail
4 Koivuhaka
high-tech, offices, service and trade
5 Tikkurila
Vantaa administrative centre and logistics
6 Hakkila
logistics and wholesale
7 Tuupakka
logistics and bonded warehouse
8 Sanomala-Myllymaki
technology production
9 Myyrmaki-Kaivoksela
technology production, logistics and trade

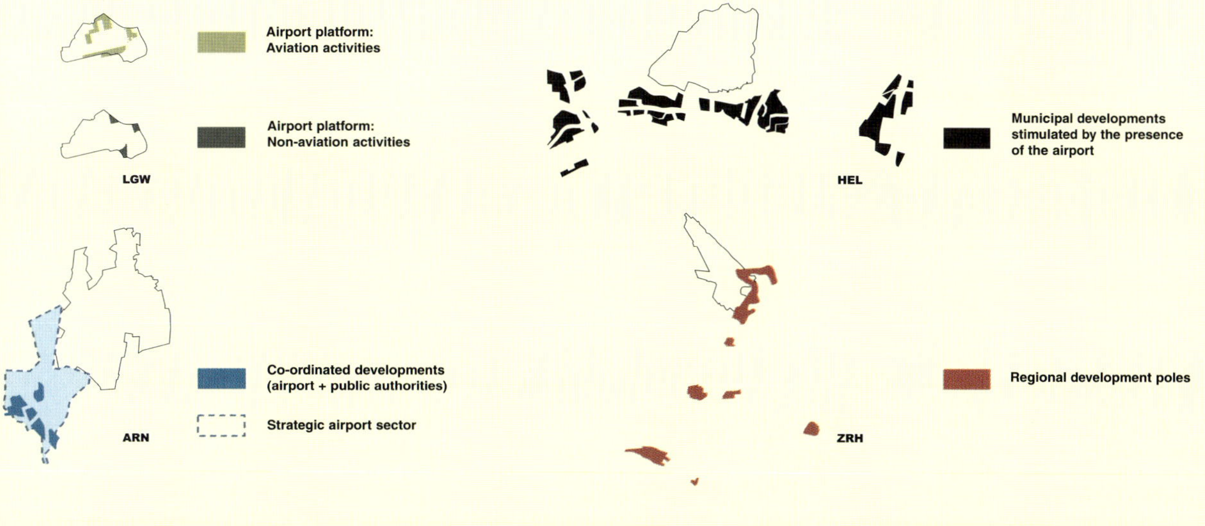

11. A city without territory

Aerial view

Oslo Airport

An airport city is "a city without a territory": there is no proper regional authority corresponding to it. The area around the airport —one of the most consistently growing parts of the metropolitan area— lies within the territory of several local authorities. These territorial conditions make it very difficult to consolidate the airport city's new role as a centre. Co-operation within this urban area has not yet been achieved on a regular basis, but has been confined to resolving common problems: task forces are often limited to discussing how best to distribute the growing noise impact of the airport.

Common development of an airport city, however, is urgently needed in order to realise the potential of, and to appease the unease caused by, the new business-oriented attitude of airports. Yet who should take the initiative in developing the airport city, if the airport area and territory is divided up between small and often still partially rural municipalities just outside the border of the city? (There are seven of these in Malpensa and five in Zurich, for example). In contrast to a city, there is no urban authority which automatically co-ordinates initiatives to profit from the opportunities appearing around the airport and its railway interchange. To develop an airport city that encompasses different parts of several municipalities is as yet unknown territory.

Spontaneity = handicap

Spontaneous, autonomous initiatives on and around airports on the part of developers, airport operators and municipalities not only compete with each other, but can also reduce the extent to which an airport region is able to benefit from the presence of a big airport. Independent initiatives make it impossible to present the crit-

ZRH

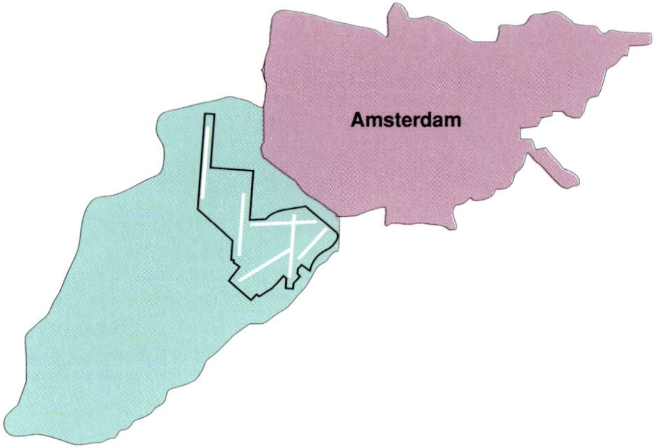

AMS

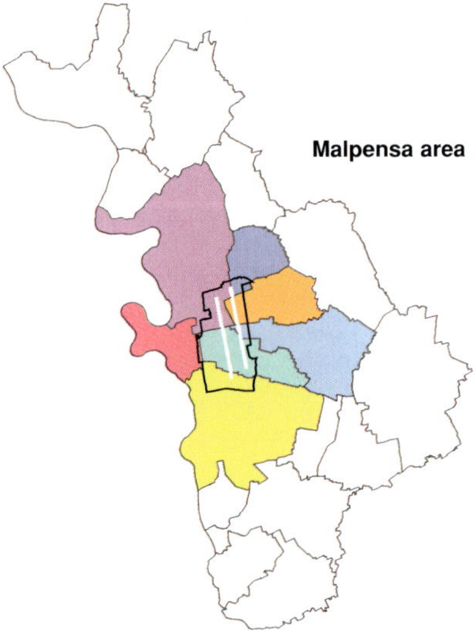

MXP

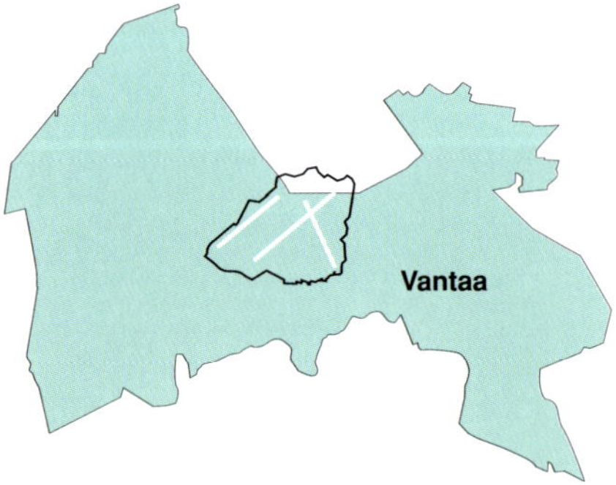

HEL

The airport city is a "city without territory". Often, this results in completely dispersed decision-making processes, and also in a kind of egocentricity on the part of each municipality with regard to the exploitation of the potential benefits in the airport area.

ical mass of adequate and sufficiently large development sites necessary when promoting the airport area for airport-related activities in the competition between European regions.

The inclination to "do it yourself", instead of "doing it together", makes common marketing almost impossible. But individual marketing is inefficient: the market demands a certain clarity as to when a particular development can be expected. An unclear profile and insecurity about investment opportunities are unappealing.

Moreover, the importance of accessibility for the overall investment climate is often overlooked. There is an inherent danger of traffic congestion around airports, even though airport city developments cannot always be held responsible for congestion on the national highways to and from the airport: they are thought to create only 3-4% of extra traffic on external roads. Transport policies, and hence investment in traffic infrastructure, lag behind the rapid accommodation of economic activities. Such an imbalance is likely to become very expensive in the long-term. As airports face suffocation due to the pressure on land use (over-development) and decreasing accessibility in their area, the allocation of extra airport-related activities becomes increasingly hazardous and speculative.

Irritation about a white spot

The new business-oriented airport concept is often still vague and protean, leaving surrounding municipalities in a state of uncertainty as to what kind of airport city development they may expect on the platform. Most disputes focus on operator strategies for developing activities with a high profit per m^2: top-notch business activities, shopping, high-tech industries, leisure and entertainment. Public authorities argue that their accommodation on the platform is not compulsory, but was once commonly held to be a monopoly

Profit

	Core business	Airport-related	Airport-oriented	Profiting of the airport image
high value/m²	terminal services: duty-free, IT-services, etc.	international logistic headquarters	international business activities (headquarters); WTC (international trade centre)	shopping ICT-business other offices
	ground handling	post & courier services test & training centres catering	hotel conference restaurants medical care centre	entertainment science park research & development education
	airplane maintenance	flower-fair EDC (europ. distribution centres) parts centre	value-added logistics (Cargo City) international exhibition centre	pharmaceutical industry high-tech industry electronic industry food industry
low value/m²	freight centres		expo centre of regional economy; large-scale, international transport & distribution	regional transport and distribution companies recreation, golf course

Close relation to air traffic — Loose relation to air traffic

- aviation activities
- undisputed relation to the airport
- once exclusively metropolitan activities

As a wide range of activities appear at European airports, it becomes urgent to discuss an adequate package of activities for the airport city.

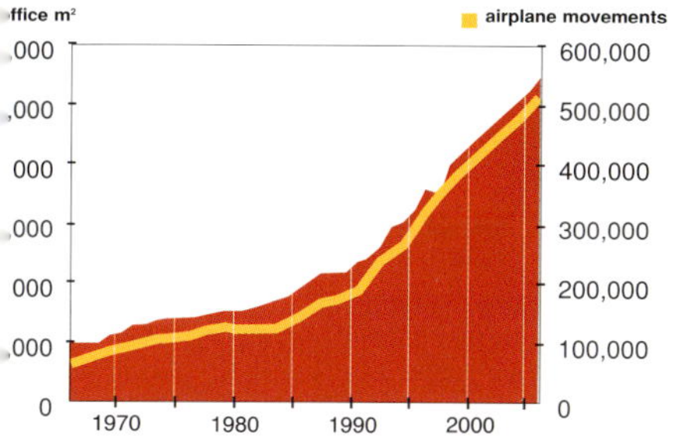

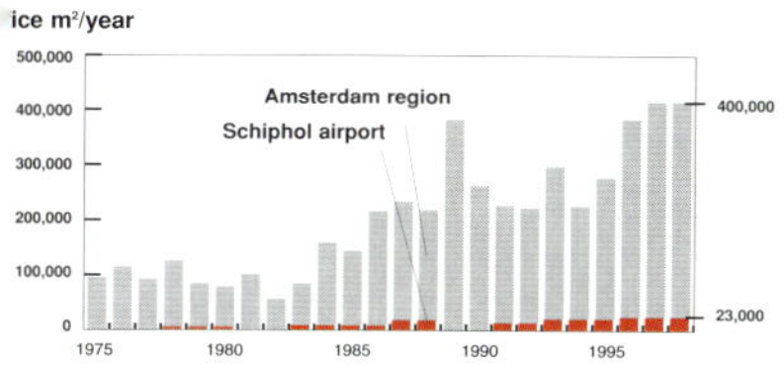

The office stock at Schiphol Airport grows at the same speed as, and is proportional to, plane movements. Compared to the m² built per year in the whole Amsterdam region, this amounts to some 5% only.

of established cities. Added to which, they fear the huge additional car traffic occasioned by the airport operators' landside development activities. The host city feels that such massive real estate development on the platform would threaten its own business parks, or even its centre.

Yet, if looked at it in a more differentiated way, if development on the platform is compared to the growth of office stock in the city as a whole —whether in AMS, FRA, BCN or VIE— the construction of floor surface at the airport amounts to only some 4% of the total annual growth of the metropolitan area. It seems reasonable, then, to consider one of the main railway stations as a site for office development, a zone of high added value with a global market-oriented programme.

The problem lies, rather, in the "white spot mentality" with which airport operators protect their territory, and which is still deeply rooted and reflected in the approach of public authorities. Irritation arises from the unclear and somewhat uncontrolled and uncontrollable conditions in the airport territory, and its exemption from being part of the common land pool of the airport area.

Laissez-faire?

As yet little has been done in a co-ordinated manner in terms of developing the airport area. Local authorities are confronted by a rapidly changing airport, one that is infinitely bigger than they themselves are in terms of territory, workforce, traffic generation and turnover. Regional authorities have hardly any tools to hand that would permit them to assume more than an advisory role on land use matters, or to work towards increased balance in the economic development of the region.

Political pressure is also exerted on the surrounding municipalities, a pressure aimed at convincing them that limiting air traffic growth would directly curtail the positive economic effects. The potential economic benefits of an airport, however, are not directly proportional to air traffic and passenger numbers. The common political argument that more aviation movement will create an automatic increase in profit can no longer be sustained. It is possible to optimise the quantity and distribution of such benefits with other means. But optimisation needs co-ordination.

Clear and specific policies in this regard —instead of a "laissez-faire" approach— make a difference. Given the lack of a larger territorial authority, land use planning seems not to be an appropriate tool. Most airport municipalities are unlikely to readily transfer this principal planning right of theirs, for part or all of their territory, to a new authority. Frankfurt is one of the few regions that has a regional land use authority. Established in the 1970s due to the urgent need for improved co-ordination between city and hinterland, this tool could once again turn out to be very useful in view of current challenges in the development of the airport area. Having said that, traditional land use and traffic planning in a region will hardly suffice for guiding an adequate distribution of economic effects.

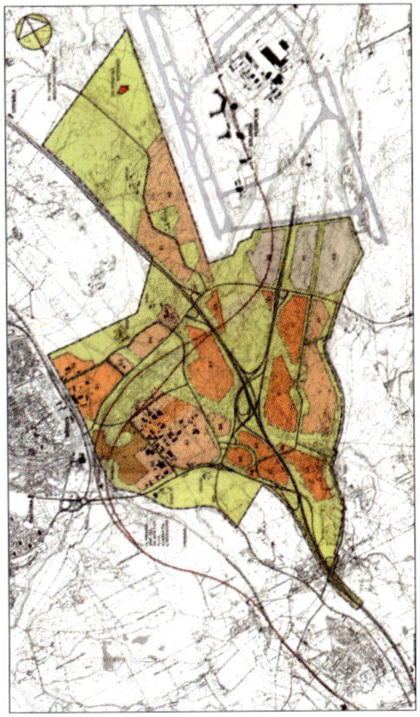

Selectivity and branding can be indispensable for success. Stockholm's Arlanda Airport is co-operating with the airport municipality Sigtuna in a common initiative: Arlandastad, an area of 593 ha right next to the airport. Ten years of trying to attract a huge variety of IT, high-tech and logistical businesses to the area have resulted in a single major peripheral shopping centre. Only now, after branding Arlandastad more precisely as being a "North European Logistical Centre NELC" does development starts to move.

New tools make a difference

New tools are required to match the exigencies of developing the "territory-less" city. Some regions have successfully begun collaborating on selectivity, co-ordinated marketing, and even development co-operation. Their experience shows that close partnerships and a clear definition of responsibilities between public authorities

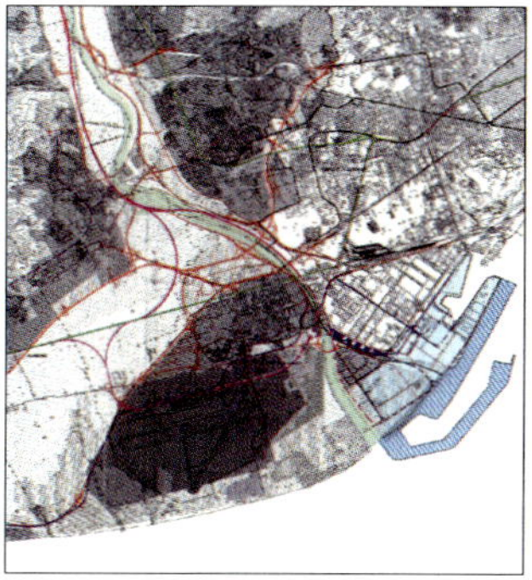

In Barcelona, the Llobregat Delta has been designated a logistical platform for the metropolitan area, intended to accommodate the spin-off of both port and airport, and to provide the required landside infrastructure.

and the airport are required to exploit the positive impact of airport growth on the regional economy, and to simultaneously guarantee the efficiency and optimum performance of the airport itself. Strategic co-operation by public/private partnerships (guided growth) is beginning to replace spontaneous development initiatives and uncontrolled growth.

Selectivity and branding

The real question is "what is developed where, and also when, in the airport area". In both good and bad times it is necessary, and at the same time advantageous, to be selective about the kind of activities admitted and accommodated on development sites in the airport surroundings. It seems obvious that a certain hierarchy between development plans in the airport area, including the operator's ambitions on the platform itself, is necessary. The fact that most development sites in the airport area are rather close together, and form part of a densely urbanised area, makes it unlikely that all of them are equally adequate candidates, in the short term, for a successful and valuable urban development. It must be possible to postpone certain developments, and give priority to others.

With site reservations for specifically airport-related activities such as logistics, sites are given a clear label. Such strict selectivity must also be based on an evaluation of the site's integration within the transport network. They are no longer just business sites, but are branded: a market advantage. In Amsterdam, Stockholm, Barcelona and Helsinki, strategic zones have been set up to provide sufficient space for logistical activities at the threshold of the airport. To establish such zones, in which development can be promoted, co-ordinated and monitored, the municipalities involved seek co-operation with airport operators and other logistical companies. The "Schiphol zone", for example — a belt of land around the airport— is exclusively geared to "activities which need to be relatively close to the airport because of their position in freight flows, and/or which are important for the operation of the airport."

Wherever synergies between several potent infrastructures are to be anticipated, the reservation of strategically favourable sites for logistical operators is important if one wants to generate economies of scale. Helsinki's "E18-TEN" corridor, linked to both airport and seaport, is promoted as just such a major logistical zone at European level. Its development is under the auspices of a specially set up "Centre of Logistical Expertise".

Being selective also means promoting sites close to the airport for activities for which airport regions compete internationally. Focussing on such a segment of activities can add to the portfolio of metropolitan regions, with their well-established centres, and it can further clarify the specific differences between these centres. A clear typecasting of the airport area is a strong marketing tool. It could be the key to establishing a regional balance.

Marketing and development co-operation

A powerful marketing strategy for the airport area is to complement selectivity by compensating for the inadequacy of traditional planning instruments in this area. Marketing, though, can also represent the airport region as a whole on a global platform. The AAA (Amsterdam Airport Area) partnership's marketing strategy includes not only the different development poles around the airport, but those of the entire urban area. The AAA demonstrates that marketing can go even further in terms of development co-ordination:

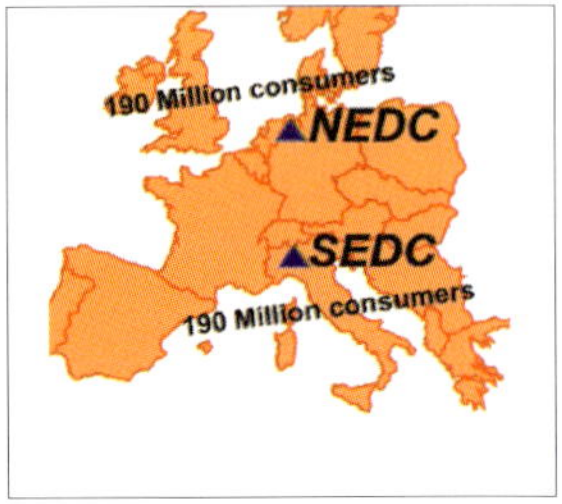

Centre Logistic BARCELONA

AMSTERDAM AIRPORT AREA

From pure brand to development co-operation.

it provides an overview of all plans, the type of activities to be realised, and gives information about development schedules.
Joint marketing replaces individual initiatives. But joint marketing is not development co-operation. It is only a stepping stone to development. With marketing alone it is not possible to overcome discrepancies between sites, and to control potential bottlenecks. To handle a specific planning context, development corporations are needed. A regional development company is not easy to establish, however: it automatically requires the co-operation of all the entities involved, and would require municipalities and the airport to partly renounce their monopoly as to land use planning on their sites.

Development within noise contours?

Public acceptance of airport development reflects the distribution of noise. It is generally lower in areas that lie beneath designated landing or takeoff routes. But acceptance is even lower if the pattern of distribution of the economic benefits of an airport is all but congruent with the noise contours. Compensation may become a major element in the attempt to balance the expansion of air traffic and in optimising the exploitation of the economic potential of an airport.
As of now, the town of Vantaa, the airport municipality in Helsinki, may be the exception in regarding its airport's noise contours as "our major problem and our major asset." Its noise contour means that a large area —almost 25% of the municipality's territory— is uncontested by other functions, and can be reserved and promoted for logistical and industrial use, to become the centrepiece of the Helsinki logistical zone along the highway corridor.

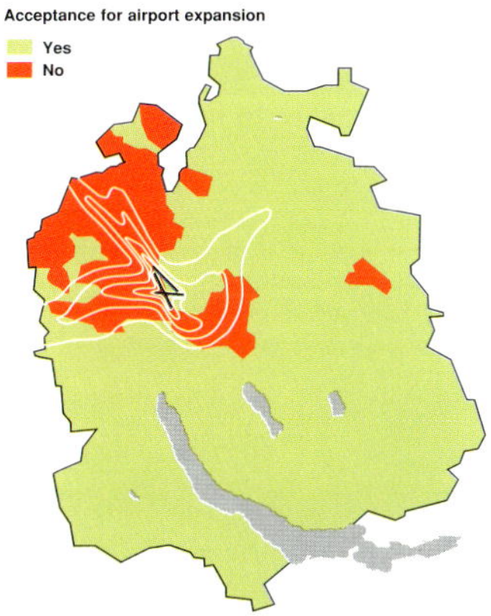

Canton of Zurich

Acceptance of airport expansion is also a question of how much noise a municipality suffers. A Canton of Zurich vote in 2000 clearly demonstrates how opposition and high noise emissions under landing and take-off routes coincide!

Provided the highway and rail corridors lie within the noise corridors, opportunities have to be grasped for locating logistical and industrial activities, but also business and recreational functions (depending on respective noise protection legislation), in these areas. Tax revenues, employment opportunities, and good integration within public transport networks function as potential compensation for noise emissions and other environmental nuisances. At HEL and ARN Airports, this is more or less simple: in both instances only one municipality is really affected, and landside infrastructures coincide with the noise zones. If several municipalities compete for business parks, or if noise-affected areas lack convenient access, it becomes a challenge to satisfy them all.

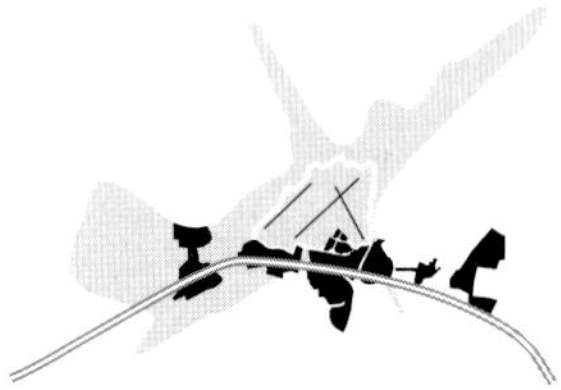

HEL-E18 corridor

In the case of Vantaa (HEL) the allocation of economic development can be attuned to the noise contours. However, the positioning of the infrastructural corridor and the noise impact do not always overlap.

AMS: a laboratory for co-operation

The Schiphol region has become a laboratory for cross-level co-operation, marketing and airport-related site development. A brief look at Schiphol's history reveals that there are no recipes for guaranteeing success. Strategies as well as partnerships have undergone several phases of "fine-tuning" in direct reaction to the state of the economy and corresponding opportunities.

The initiative — In the late 1980s the province of north Holland and Schiphol Airport were deeply worried about the rapid development of business sites on the land around the airport, limiting its flexibility for expansion, and threatening its accessibility. They were concerned that municipalities would permit fast and uncontrolled site development, when put under pressure by developers who had managed to buy land around the airport. In 1987, together with Haarlemmermeer airport municipality, the city of Amsterdam and the National Investment Bank (supplying funding), they set up a "Schiphol zone" with land from both Amsterdam and Haarlemmermeer.

"Bestuursforum Schiphol" and "Schiphol Area Development Company": a common forum for mediation and joint real estate development to compensate for the lack of co-ordination in the airport area.

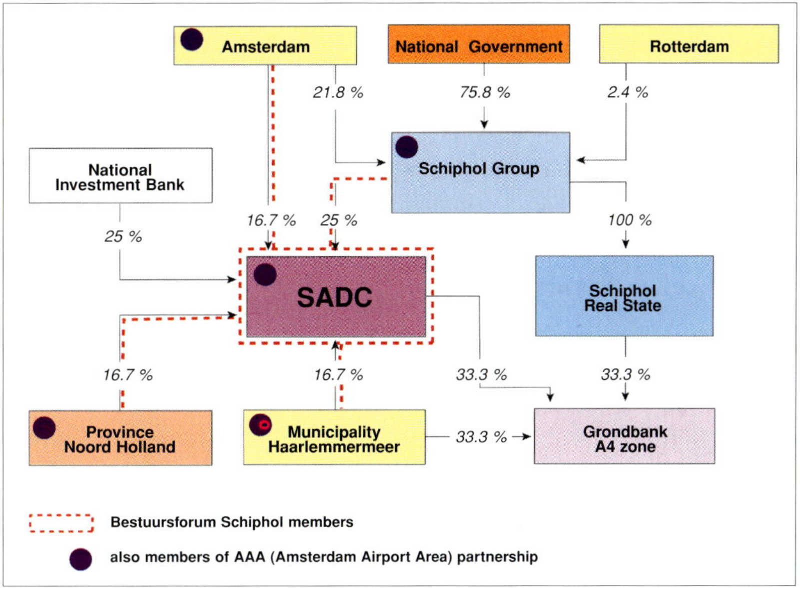

The AAA or Amsterdam Airport Area: along with development co-operation within the SADC (yellow sites), another "umbrella" organisation, the AAA, has been set up for the joint marketing and promotion of all major development sites in the Amsterdam region (red sites). Under the chairmanship of the SADC, it pools information on real estate development, regarding availability, development priority and programming.

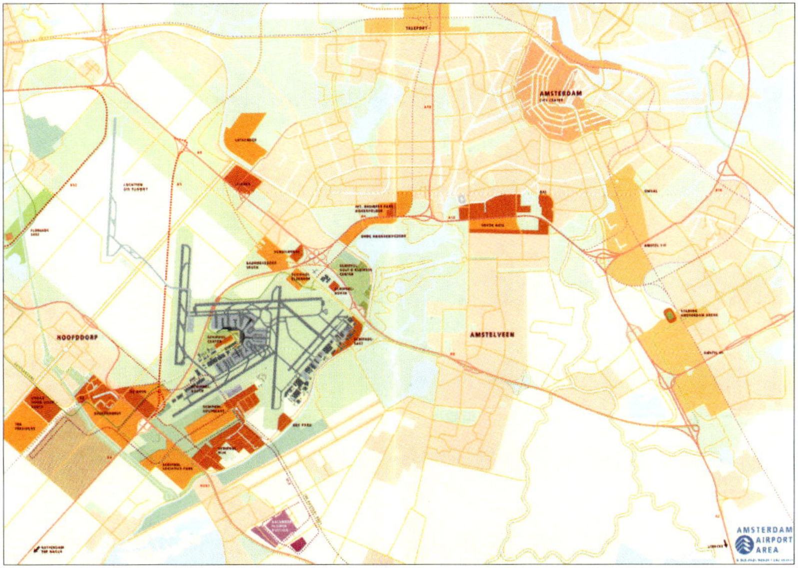

Schiphol Centre: an airport city in the making.

Amsterdam's southern periphery —the "cash corridor" of the Netherlands— is to be built on top of a vast set of infrastructures: an ambitious plan, for a still huge gap in the city.

The zone is a land-pool within which a common and independent land development company, the SADC (Schiphol Area Development Company), was to develop, promote and sell land for logistical companies and the offices related to them (similar to the Arlandastad Company at Stockholm Arlanda Airport). The contract charged the SADC with applying selection criteria as to potential clients: a set percentage of the activities of businesses was to serve either air cargo, or air passengers.

Notwithstanding the competition with major developers in the area, the SADC managed over the years to buy considerable tracts of land within the Schiphol zone, and successfully attracted international firms, in particular a major share of the European distribution centres of different Japanese and US companies.

A period of insignificance — With the economic boom of the 1990s, and in view of the opportunities for dedicated office development, the partners focussed more and more on their own affairs. The SADC's importance gradually declined.

The municipality of Haarlemmermeer launched Beukenhorst, a competing, but highly successful, business park of 350,000 m^2, with a reserve of another 250,000 m^2. The municipality was less selective than the SADC with respect to the airport-relatedness of the businesses moving in. At the same time, Schiphol Airport started to develop business sites on its own territory, for example the "Schiphol Centre", the landside core area between terminals. The logical next step was to set up its own real estate company, Schiphol Real Estate (SRE).

To make the situation even more complex, all kinds of special partnerships were established for developing sites in the airport surroundings, with the SADC only partially involved. A strip along the

A4 highway just south of the airport, for instance, will be developed by the SRE, the SADC and the municipality of Haarlemmermeer, each holding a 33% share.

Too little guidance? — Such a strong economic development to the south of the airport, and major logistical and office development on the airport itself, perturbed the city of Amsterdam. It saw its own ambitious plans for the Zuid-As threatened by the equally attractive, but cheaper, sites at the airport, which also had the advantage of shorter development times. With airport privatisation around the corner, the city of Amsterdam intended to exchange a 12% package of its airport shares for land on the airport territory —on Haarlemmermeer municipality's terrain, let it be said— in order to be able to exert more direct influence on the development of the on-airport commercial programme.

At the same time, Haarlemmermeer found it increasingly difficult to manage and control international business development all alone.

The revival of the SADC — In this situation, the SADC has once more been recognised as the ideal co-ordinating tool. As its original land reserves are almost used up, the land-pool will be expanded to also include parts of the Zuid-As, the advantage for Amsterdam being that these sites are in its own hands. On these new sites, the SADC is responsible for co-ordination and development guidance; its activities will no longer involve any financial participation in development, however. Both Haarlemmermeer and Amsterdam do not want Schiphol Airport to become involved, via its stake in the SADC, in areas outside the Schiphol zone.

The SADC has changed. It has evolved from an organisation for promoting the Schiphol region to a wider co-operative effort for relieving mistrust and competition. The challenge, today, is to co-ordinate the urban development of an area that, due to the airport and the resulting concentration of infrastructural transport networks, has become the most dynamic development area in the Netherlands.

The airport territory itself is not part of the land-pool and has therefore remained a bone of contention. The airport operator needs to specify the business sectors targeted in its conception of “creating airport cities”, in order to more clearly distinguish what it is attempting to accommodate on its own development sites, thereby responding to, and trying to alleviate, the concerns of local and regional authorities.

An unusual planning task

Aerial view

Copenhagen Airport

The bigger the airport, the bigger the urban territory affected; the bigger the likely discrepancies with the local territory; the smaller the possibilities of influence on the part of local and regional authorities. With the exception of Paris, Madrid or Milan —which seek to avoid conflicts by placing new airports in less densely populated areas away from the city— airports are here to stay. The demand for co-ordination and co-operation will increase, and the parameters of airport planning will have to be redefined. So far, however, urban planners have been unwilling to grasp and harness the power of the airport in developing the metropolitan area. If the airport is not a city in itself, it is a vital constituent of the city as a whole.

A mixture of benefits and nuisance

Airport development is a controversial mixture of benefits and nuisance. In globally operating markets, airports have become critical assets in the competition between regions. But in order to guarantee flexibility for a meaningful expansion of capacity, airports generate an unprecedented demand for land. They disburse ever-larger noise carpets over the territory, making local development problematic. As a consequence, both environmental nuisance and the ambition to minimise the adverse effects of airport development dominate the local political agenda. As against this, the potential benefits of air traffic are simplified to the level of rhetorical statistics on the favourable economic effects of air traffic growth —abstract job numbers and GDP millions. Not surprisingly, these respective positions are most firmly rooted.

This is too narrow a view. Airport regions are not just land under sufferance. Developing an airport city —the quality accommodation of airport spin-off— and rebuilding the airport railway station as an interchange node in landside transport are not only part of recent airport thinking. They are the two aspects of airport development that offer an opportunity to create added value for the disadvantaged parties and to compensate for nuisance.

For the airport, this means stepping back from going it all alone. Now that commercial real estate development has become part and parcel of airport operation, and that the privatisation of formerly national airport operators is on its way, airports become more exigent players, but also more immediate partners for the regions. If an airport city is built, it ought not to remain the sole venture of an airport operator, but must become an integral part of the whole region. If accessibility to the airport is improved, then accessibility throughout the region can probably be improved along with it: an interchange node requires a different logic than point-to-point access to the terminals, and it thus presents new opportunities.

The comeback of infrastructure

Enclosure of the airport within the metropolitan area makes integral strategic planning —a combination of land use and transport planning— indispensable. The development of transport infrastructures and of real estate in the airport area cannot be looked at separately any more. Uncontrolled exploitation of the airport's attractiveness has often raced ahead of infrastructural investment. This is disconcerting, as it affects the primary need to keep the airport itself accessible. And access is not only vital for the airport: it is also a prerequisite for development. It guarantees the overall investment climate and attractiveness of an area. If bottlenecks appear, business companies are the first to leave.

As desirable as such fully integrated concepts are, they are undermined by the fact that responsibilities for land use and infrastructure planning are usually split between local and regional authorities. Due to this segregation, infrastructure has for too long been a more or less delayed response to the growth of metropolitan areas; a more or less urgent supplement to economic development. The potential for guiding and promoting development through infrastructural investment has to be recognised. More than ever before, infrastructure is a strategic tool that regains a central position in spatial and urban planning.

Airports are the central stations of the 21st century. The growth of airport cities and the evolution of interchange nodes at airports are interdependent concepts. But often airport cities are developed where there is space for unhindered construction, not where connections are good. An opportunity is being missed here. For example, building the airport administration or any other office centre directly on top of the airport interchange rather than elsewhere will encourage an additional 5% of employees to leave their car at home, as Frankfurt Airport showed in relation to its AIRail terminal. Strategies like these, which go beyond facilitating access for passengers alone and focus on the access quality of the entire airport city, should not be underestimated. Improving landside accessibility is an ongoing battle for a few percent of extra public transport customers that has to be fought for via heavy investment in the airport region. The approximately 9km-long and 220 million-Euro Marjaline, which is to link up with Helsinki Airport, is expected to generate a 3% increase in the share of public transport to the airport; Frankfurt's "Regionaltangente West", a 1.1% increase. Most of these new rail lines have no more than one stop at the airport. Which other bit of the city would be served in this way?

An unusual planning task

A contemporary airport requires a different logic to that of expanding terminals and hangars. The transformation of an airport into an airport city is as ambitious —and maybe even more daring— as any central station redevelopment. Yet airport planning —and thus planning an airport city— is no ordinary planning task! It is a particularly difficult one, since everything is on the move. An airport is subject to continual transformation; there is an extreme development dynamic on the platform and in its immediate surroundings. Airport planning is confronted by the severe handicap of inadequate territorial boundaries. The potential partnerships and responsibilities for developing an airport city together are not yet clearly defined. The airport operator claims two tasks for itself: the public responsibility of "running an airport", and the private interests of "developing the airfield". The Airport City concept has not been patented by the airport operator, however. The Barcelona experience has shown that the creation and management of an airport city is the shared responsibility of both airport operators and public authorities.

Airport city planning moves away from purely "technical airport planning" to include aspects of the urban planning process. An airport's classic infrastructure plans are insufficient for handling the complex organisation of the airport landside. And so are public land use plans: they fall short when it comes to the operational requirements of an airport. The challenge is to merge these different planning cultures.

Airport planning is highly specific, having a double agenda and a split reality to be satisfied. It has become a delicate balancing act between conflicting interests: providing space for manoeuvre for the airport infrastructure, and eventually exploiting opportunities for non-aviation development around the interchange. At the core of an airport city there is an airport with all its problems and its security needs. In a city, expansion and transformation are neither as rapid, nor as extensive, nor as radical, and its traffic networks are stable by comparison.

An airport is not simply an airport any more. But neither is it just a city.

Glossary and abbreviations

AAA
Amsterdam Airport Area

AENA
Aeropuertos Españoles y Navegación Aérea, Spain-CAA

Airport area
Area adjacent to and including the airport, the transformation of which is directly related to the airport development

Airport city
Definition p. 70

Airport interchange
Definition p. 131

Airport platform
Territory within the airport perimeter

Airport product
New notion of an airport based on a comprehensive business orientation (airside and landside development)

Airport region
A region containing an international airport

Airport-oriented activities
Activities that choose the airport or the region to settle because of the image and function of the airport as a regional and international interface (interchange node) and as a business location. They profit from the regional and international accessibility of the airport. The price of the land, not the activities' relation to air traffic, will automatically determine which of them will be able to settle close to the airport

Airport-related activities
Activities with a direct functional relation to or dependence on air traffic (freight, passengers) and airport operation, e.g. logistical and distribution activities or hotels. They choose to locate at the airport or in its surroundings due to its (inter)national competitiveness

AMS
Amsterdam Schiphol Airport; Province North Holland

ARN
Stockholm Arlanda Airport; Stockholm County, Sigtuna Municipality

Authorities
Local and/or regional public authorities

Aviation activities
Core business, operational or aeronautical activities: activities that are part of the technical operation of the airport, directly supporting the air traffic function

BAA
British Airports Authority

BCN
Barcelona Airport; Barcelona Area Metropolitana

BR
Barcelona Regional: metropolitan agency for urbanism and infrastructures

CAA
Civil Airports Administration or Civil Aviation Administration, State administrations of airports and aeronautical matters

CDG
Charles de Gaulle Airport; Paris, Île-de-France

Collaboration
Partnership

Core business
Aviation, operational or platform-bound activities which have a direct functional relation with the airport, the activities of the "core business"

CPH
Copenhagen Airport; Region of Öresund

CS
Central station

DB
Deutsche Bahn AG, German National Railway Company

FRA
Frankfurt Airport; Umlandverband Frankfurt

HEL
Helsinki Vantaa Airport; Helsinki Metropolitan Area, City of Vantaa

HST
High Speed Train

Hub
An airport with a substantial share of transfer between intercontinental flights and continental flights/HST. The increasing amount of transfer passengers in these airports and consequent higher aircraft occupancy rates

lead to the feasibility of additional services and routes to and from this airport. One expects that there will be place for 4-6 hubs in Europe

Hybrid airport
The hybrid airport is a typology developed and designed by the authors for a recent European airport competition

IC
InterCity train

ICE
InterCity Express (German High Speed Train)

Interchange node
Interconnection of different means and levels of transport which allows for transfer between them

JFK
John F. Kennedy Airport; New York

LGW
London Gatwick Airport; West Sussex County

LHR
London Heathrow Airport; City of London

Metropolitan area, metropolitan region
Conurbation, city region

MRE
Malpensa Real Estate

Municipality
Local government area within a region

MXP
Milan Malpensa Airport; Regione Lombardia

Noise contour
Zone which indicates the noise level generated by air traffic on the ground. It is used to indicate zones within which certain type of land use (noise-sensitive) is to be restricted

Non-aviation activities
Non-operational or non-aeronautical activities, such as airport-related activities and airport-oriented activities. They are complementing aviation activities as ingredients of the airport city

Off-airport
Beyond the airport perimeter

On-airport
Within the airport perimeter

Operator
Airport operator

Pax
Air traffic passengers

Pole
Centre or concentration of activity or development

PPP
Public private partnership

PT
Public transport

Regional hub
An interchange node which acquires a crucial position in regional networks. The same principle that makes an airport a hub (see Hub) also makes an airport railway station a regional hub

SADC
Schiphol Area Development Company

SEA
Società Esercizi Aeroportuali, Milanese airport authority

SME
Small and medium-sized enterprises

SNCF
Société Nationale des Chemins de Fer Français, French National Railway Company

SRE
Schiphol Real Estate

Tangential route
Circular route, ring road

TEN
Trans-European network

Territory
Land owned or administered

TGV
Train à Grande Vitesse (French High Speed Train)

Travelator
Horizontal escalator to bridge long walking distances, used in airports, shopping malls or train stations.

UVF
Umlandverband Frankfurt, today PVFRM Planungsverband Frankfurt RheinMain

VIE
Vienna Airport; Province and City of Vienna

ZRH
Zurich Airport; Canton of Zurich

Bibliography

Representatives of the following entities have kindly contributed information in the form of discussions, documents and support, and with their time and insights, during the case-study visits to the nine airport regions:

AMS: Corus, SRE, SADC, Provincie Noord Holland, Buck Consultants, VROM
ARN: SCAA, Sigtuna municipality, Stockholm County Council RTK, City of Stockholm, Arlandastad Company
BCN: El Prat municipality, Barcelona Regional, AENA
FRA: FAG, City of Frankfurt, UVF Umlandverband Frankfurt
HEL: City of Vantaa, CAA Helsinki, National Road Administration, Helsinki Metropolitan Area Council YTV
LGW: West Sussex County Council, Borough of Crawley
MXP: Regione Lombardia, SEA, municipalities of Gallarate, Busto-Arsizio, Ferno-Lonate Pozzolo, Vizzola Ticino, CLAS, Centro Studi PIM
ZRH: Unique Zurich Airport, Canton of Zurich

AMS
- *Building at Airports 1995-2000*, Schiphol Real Estate, Schiphol, 2000
- *Business City Schiphol / Schiphol Real Estate*, Schiphol Real Estate, Schiphol, 1999
- *Creating Airport Cities*, Schiphol Group, Schiphol, 1999
- Dierikx, Marc *et. al.*, *Schiphol Haven / Station / Knooppunt sinds 1916*, Walburg Pers, Zutphen, 1999
- H+N+S, DRO and DHV, *Locatiestudie Schiphol*, TNLI, Utrecht / Amsterdam / Amersfoort, 1998
- Kloos, Maarten and De Maar, Birgitte, *Schiphol Architecture: Innovative Airport Design*, ARCAM / Architectura & Natura Press, Amsterdam, 1996
- *Partiële herziening Streekplan ANZKG - Haarlemmermeer / Schiphol*, Provincie Noord-Holland, Haarlem, 1995

ARN
- Bana 3– *en projektbeskrivning*, Luftfartsverket, Stockholm, 1999
- *RUFS Regionplan 2000*, Regionplane- och Trafikkontoret Stockholm County Council, Stockholm, 2000
- *Stockholm - Arlanda Airport*, Luftfartsverket, Stockholm-Arlanda, 1996
- *What Characterizes a Big Airport*, Länstyrelsen Stockholms Län, Stockholm, 1985

BCN
- Alemany, Joan, *El Plan Delta III– Análisis económico de las grandes infraestructuras*, Ajuntament de Barcelona, Barcelona, 1996
- *Aeropuerto de Barcelona– Desarrollo e integración territorial*, Barcelona Regional, Barcelona, 1996
- *Barcelona New Projects*, Ajuntament de Barcelona / Barcelona Regional, Barcelona, 1999
- *El finançament de les infrastructures metropolitanes de Barcelona 2000-2004-2009*, Barcelona Regional, Barcelona, 1999
- *Informe sobre la proposta de Pla Director de l'Aeroport de Barcelona de Juliol de 1999*, Barcelona Regional, Barcelona, 1999
- *Integración territorial del Aeropuerto de Barcelona– Propuestas de accesibilidad y desarrollo urbano del entorno*, AENA/Barcelona Regional/INECO, Barcelona, 1996
- *Plan Director del Aeropuerto de Barcelona*, Aeropuerto de Barcelona, Barcelona, 2000

FRA
- *Drittes Kolloquium Luftverkehr - Grossflughäfen auf dem Weg zu urbanen Zentren*, Technische Universität Darmstadt, Darmstadt, 1996
- Meyer, Jens, *Überbauung AIRail Terminal. Benchmark-Studie*, Flughafen Frankfurt/Main AG, Frankfurt, 1999
- *Report on Urban Development*, Stadt Frankfurt am Main, Frankfurt, 1995
- *Sechstes Kolloquium Luftverkehr - Der Ausbau des Frankfurter Flughafens - eine Notwendigkeit für die Region?*, TU Darmstadt, Darmstadt, 1999
- *Verkehrsknotenpunkt Flughafen Frankfurt - Für die Zukunft der Region Rhein-Main*, Deutsche Bahn AG/ Flughafen Frankfurt Main AG/Rhein Main Verkehrsverbund GmbH/Stadt Frankfurt am Main, Frankfurt, 1998
- *Vision 2000plus, Generalausbauplan 1995*, Flughafen Frankfurt Main AG, Frankfurt, 1995

HEL
- *Aviapolis - A New Business Park Next to the Helsinki-Vantaa Airport*, City of Vantaa, Helsinki, 1999

- *Helsinki Metropolitan Area Transport System Plan PLJ 1998*, Helsinki Metropolitan Area Council, Helsinki, 1999
- *The Helsinki Metropolitan Area Vision 2020*, Helsinki Metropolitan Area Council, Helsinki, 1999

LGW
- *Airport Transport Forums– Good Practice Guide*, DETR Department of the Environment, Transport and the Regions, London, 2000
- *Crawley Borough - Local Plan 2000*, Crawley Borough Council, Crawley, 2000
- *Gatwick Airport Transport Strategy 2000-2008*, BAA Gatwick, Gatwick, 2000
- *The "Provisional" Local Transport Plan for West Sussex*, West Sussex County Council, Chichester, 1999
- *West Sussex Structure Plan*, West Sussex County Council, Chichester, 1998

MXP
- *Piano territoriale dell'Area Malpensa– norme speciali per l'aerostazione intercontinentale Malpensa 2000*, Bollettino Ufficiale della Regione Lombardia, No. 94 bis Regione Lombardia, Milan, 1999
- *Studio di pianificazione AlpTransit Sud Fase C*, Bundesamt für Verkehr, Bern, 1999
- *Studio sul sistema aeroportuale Lombarda sulla rete degli aeroporti minori e sui servizi di elitrasporto, Final Report*, IRER/Regione Lombardia, Milan, 2000
- Zucchetti, Roberto, *Malpensa: A New Intercontinental Hub*, Gruppo CLAS, Milan, 1998

VIE
- "Realisierungswettbewerb Städtebauliche Konzeption Flughafen Wien", in *Architekturjournal Wettbewerbe*, 193-195, Kommerzialrat J. R. Bahula, Vienna, 2000
- *Step by Step: Urban Development Plan/ The new Traffic Concept*, Vienna Urban Development and Planning, Vienna, 1995
- *Vision 2015*, VIE Vienna airport, Vienna, 1998

ZRH
- Oliva, Carl et alt., *Liberalisierung im Luftverkehr: Folgen für die Schweiz*, Nationales Forschungsprogramm NFP 41, Bern, 2000
- Prognos/Emch & Berger, *Flughafen Zürich: Erhebung zum landseitigen Verkehr und Motivforschung zur Verkehrsmittelwahl*, Amt für Verkehr/Unique Zürich Airport, Zurich, 1999
- *Raumbeobachtung Kanton Zürich, Siedlungsentwicklung*, Amt für Raumordnung und Vermessung Kanton Zürich, Zurich, 1998
- *SIL– Sachplan Infrastruktur der Luftfahrt*, Bundesamt für Zivil-Luftfahrt, Bern, 2000
- *Flughafen Zürich Masterplan 92*, Volkswirtschafts-Direktion Kanton Zürich, Zurich, 1992

General
- Augé, Marc, *Non-Lieux, Introduction à une antropologie de la surmodernité*, Seuil, Paris, 1992; (English version: *Non-Places: Introduction to an Anthropology of Supermodernity*, Verso, London, 1995)
- Berthon, Etienne and Bringand, Flore, *Airport City and Regional Embeddedness- Final Report*, IAURIF/COFAR/ADP, Paris, 2001
- *deArchitect (*Dossier 7- Luchthaventerminals), The Hague, 1998
- DEGW/Buck Consultants International, *The impact of High Speed Trains on Urban Centres*, Ministerie van VROM, The Hague, 1998
- Gaudriault, Claude *et al., L'impact économique des aéroports*, Région d'Île-de-France/Direction Générale de l'Aviation Civile, Paris, 1995
- Husson, Jean Louis *et al., Regions and Airports, Partners for Sustainable Prosperity*, Airport Regions Conference, Barcelona, 1999
- Navarre, Danièle, *Le Développement de la grande vitesse ferroviaire en Europe*, Conseil Régional d'Île-de-France, Paris, 1999
- Robusté, Francesc and Julià, Jordi, *Promoting Public Transport at Airports*, Airport Regions Conference, Barcelona, 1999
- *Zones aéroportuaires, Plates-formes multimodales*, DREIF/Mission Roissy, Paris, 1993
- Zucchetti, Roberto and Baccelli, Oliviero, *Aeroporti e Territorio*, EGEA, Milano, 2001
- Zukowsky, John (ed.), *Building for Air Travel*, The Art Institute of Chicago/Prestel Verlag, New York, 1996

Credits

Where not mentioned otherwise, the illustrations have been produced by Güller Güller architecture urbanism and are © 2002 Güller Güller architecture urbanism.

p. 12, background: Planungsverband Frankfurt RheinMain; p.13, background: Provincie Noord Holland; p. 14, background: Ordnance Survey, UK; p. 15, background: Amt für Raumordnung und Vermessung Kanton Zürich/Baudepartement Kanton Aargau, Abteilung Raumplanung; p. 16, background: Centro Studi, PIM; p. 17, background: Barcelona Regional; p. 18, background: HUR- Greater Copenhagen Authority; p. 19, background: Regionplane- och trafikkontoret, Stockholm County Council; p. 21, background: City of Vantaa; p.22, Unique; p.31 left, background: ARV Kanton Zürich; p. 31 right, background: RTK Stockholm County Council; p.32, background: Amt für Raumordnung des Kanton Zürich; p.36, CAA Arlanda; p. 40 left, background: Ordnance Survey, UK; p. 40 right, background: Regionplane- och trafikkontoret, Stockholm County Council; p. 41 top, background: Centro Studi, PIM; p. 41 bottom, background: Barcelona Regional; p. 43, London City Airport; p. 46, KLM aerocarto-Arnhem; p. 50 from top to bottom and from left to right, Schiphol Group, CAA Arlanda, AENA, Fraport, BAA, CAA Helsinki, SEA, Vienna Airport plc, Unique Airport Zurich; p. 58, City of Vantaa; p. 63, KLM aerocarto- Arnhem; p. 72, City of Vantaa; p. 73, background: City of Vantaa; p. 74, BAA Gatwick; p. 80 top, Barcelona Regional; p. 80 bottom, BAA Gatwick; p. 83, Planpartner AG; p. 84, ING / ADP; p. 91 top, Aerophoto-Shiphol; p. 91 bottom, Nicholas Grimshaw Partners Ltd.; p. 92, Vienna Airport plc; p. 97 top, Schiphol Group; p. 97 bottom, Benthem Crouwel Architekten BV bna; p. 98, Vienna Airport plc; p. 99, Baumschlager&Eberle, Itten+Brechbühl; pp. 101-102, FAG Flughafen Frankfurt Main AG; pp. 103-104, Güller Güller architecture urbanism/Studio Sputnik with Lea+Elliott, ABT adviseurs bv, BBN adviseurs bv, H+N+S landschapsarchitecten bv; p. 108, Tavisa; p. 115, AENA; p. 119 right, background: Planungsverband Frankfurt RheinMain; p. 119 left, background: Provincie Noord Holland; p. 120 top left, background: Ordnance Survey, UK; p. 120 top right, background: Amt für Raumordnung und Vermessung Kanton Zürich/Baudepartement Kanton Aargau, Abteilung Raumplanung; p. 120 bottom left, background: Centro Studi, PIM; p. 120 bottom right, background: Barcelona Regional; p. 121 top left, background: Regionplane- och trafikkontoret, Stockholm County Council; p. 121 bottom left, background: City of Vantaa; p. 122, Foto Fraport AG; p. 129, FAG Flughafen Frankfurt Main AG; p. 133, Helsinki Metropolitan Area; p. 134, ZVV Zürcher Verkehrsverbund; p. 136, BAA Gatwick; p. 137, Unique Airport Zurich; p. 140, SEA; p. 146, background: Amsterdam Airport Area; p. 149, background: Centro Studi PIM; p. 152, Centro Studi PIM; p.153 top, background: Bundesamt für Kartographie und Geodäsie; p. 153 bottom, background: Topografische Dienst Emmen; p. 154 top, background: Ordnance Survey; p. 154 bottom, background: Bundesamt für Landestopographie; p. 155 top, background: Istituto geografico militare; p. 155 bottom, background: Institut Cartogràfic de Catalunya; p. 156 top, background: Lantmäteriverket; p. 156 bottom, background: Bundesamt für Eich- und Vermessungswesen; p. 157, background: Maanmittauslaitos Lantmäteriverket; p. 158, Oslo Airport; p. 166, Arlandastad Company; p. 167, Generalitat de Catalunya; p. 168 from top to bottom, SEA, North European Logistic Hi-Tech Centre, Barcelona Centre Logístic, Amsterdam Airport Area; p. 171 bottom, Amsterdam Airport Area; p. 172 top, Aerophoto-Shiphol; p. 172 bottom, GBR Grondbedrijf Amsterdam; p. 176, Jan Kofod Winther.

Acknowledgments

We wish to thank Peter Güller and Jordi Julià i Sort for their valuable input and critical encouragement during our research, as well as our collaborators Clara Prosdocimo and Frederik Lyth for their great help in making this book possible.
We would also like to thank the members of the ARC representing the airport regions studied for providing much of the information used: J. Julià i Sort (Barcelona Regional); E. Bieber (Umlandverband Frankfurt); H. Brattström and W. Jansson (RTK Stockholm County Council, and Luftfartverket); L. Harju and M. Holopainen (City of Vantaa, Helsinki); R. Jones (West Sussex County Council, London Gatwick); P. Lenna (Regione Lombardia, Milan-Malpensa); and H. Semela (Stadtplanung Wien).

Biography

The architects **Mathis Güller** (1968) and **Michael Güller** (1970) approach the changing conditions in the making of cities from an unexpected and integral point of view. They explore and challenge the contemporary field of urban planning and suggest a fresh and comprehensive planning culture that combines the requirements and possibilities of architecture, urban design and infrastructure planning. Through their ongoing co-operation with economists, marketing specialists, traffic engineers, and even philosophers, they have attained a high degree of flexibility when approaching a wide range of projects and extracting the particular essence and potential of each task.

In 1999 they founded **Güller Güller architecture urbanism**. Operating out of both Rotterdam (Holland) and Zurich (Switzerland), the company works towards locally defined concepts, exploiting complementarities between the specific planning context and the partners' experience in these two countries and in many others.

Their recent urban planning projects are as diverse as a competition design for a new terminal for Frankfurt Airport, quality guidelines for Schiphol Airport City, the urban integration of a new underground highway for Zurich, the spatial and economic impact of Zurich airport, strategies for long term planning provisions in this airport region, interregional co-operation for city networks in Bosnia, and a winning design catalyzing urban renewal for the Lausanne Garden Festival 2004. Their research into urban development around international airports for the ARC (2000) forms the basis of much of their involvement in airport issues.

www.ggau.net

		size	passengers in millions 2000	transfer in % 2000	freight in million tons 2000	employees 2000		runways
HEL		1,500 ha	10.01	10%	0.08	10,000	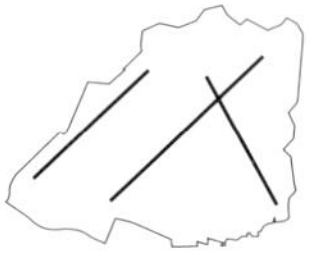	3
LGW		674 ha	32.1	32%	0.32	28,000	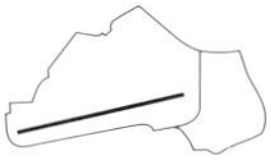	1
MXP		1,220 ha	20.72	31%	0.29	15,000	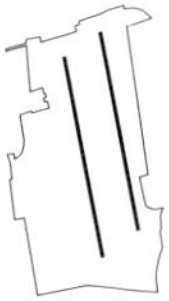	2
VIE	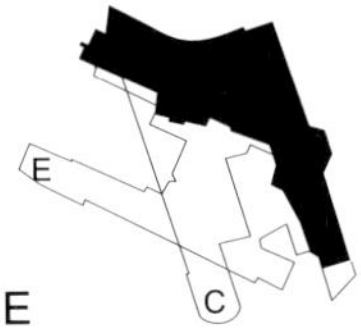	1,000 ha	11.94	27%	0.18	12,316	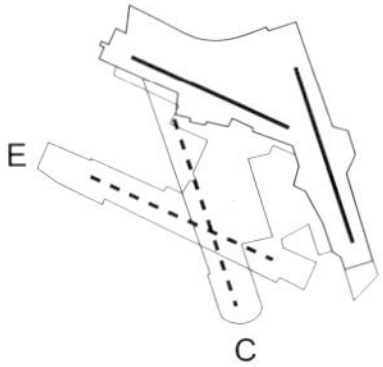	2+1
ZRH		781 ha	22.63	44%	0.39	21,000		3